THE ULTIMATE TYPE 2 DIABETES UK COOKBOOK FOR BEGINNERS

1200 Days of Healthy and Delicious Recipes for Type 2 Diabetes Newly Diagnosed With the Complete Guide to the Diabetic Diet | Full Color Pictures Version

BROOKE SMITH

Copyright© 2022 By Brooke Smith Rights Reserved

This book is copyright protected. It is only for personal use. You cannot amend, distribute, sell, use, quote or paraphrase any part of the content within this book, without the consent of the author or publisher.

Under no circumstances will any blame or legal responsibility be held against the publisher, or author, for any damages, reparation, or monetary loss due to the information contained within this book, either directly or indirectly.

Disclaimer Notice:

Please note the information contained within this document is for educational and entertainment purposes only. All effort has been executed to present accurate, up to date, reliable, complete information. No warranties of any kind are declared or implied. Readers acknowledge that the author is not engaged in the rendering of legal, financial, medical or professional advice. The content within this book has been derived from various sources. Please consult a licensed professional before attempting any techniques outlined in this book.

By reading this document, the reader agrees that under no circumstances is the author responsible for any losses, direct or indirect, that are incurred as a result of the use of the information contained within this document, including, but not limited to, errors, omissions, or inaccuracies.

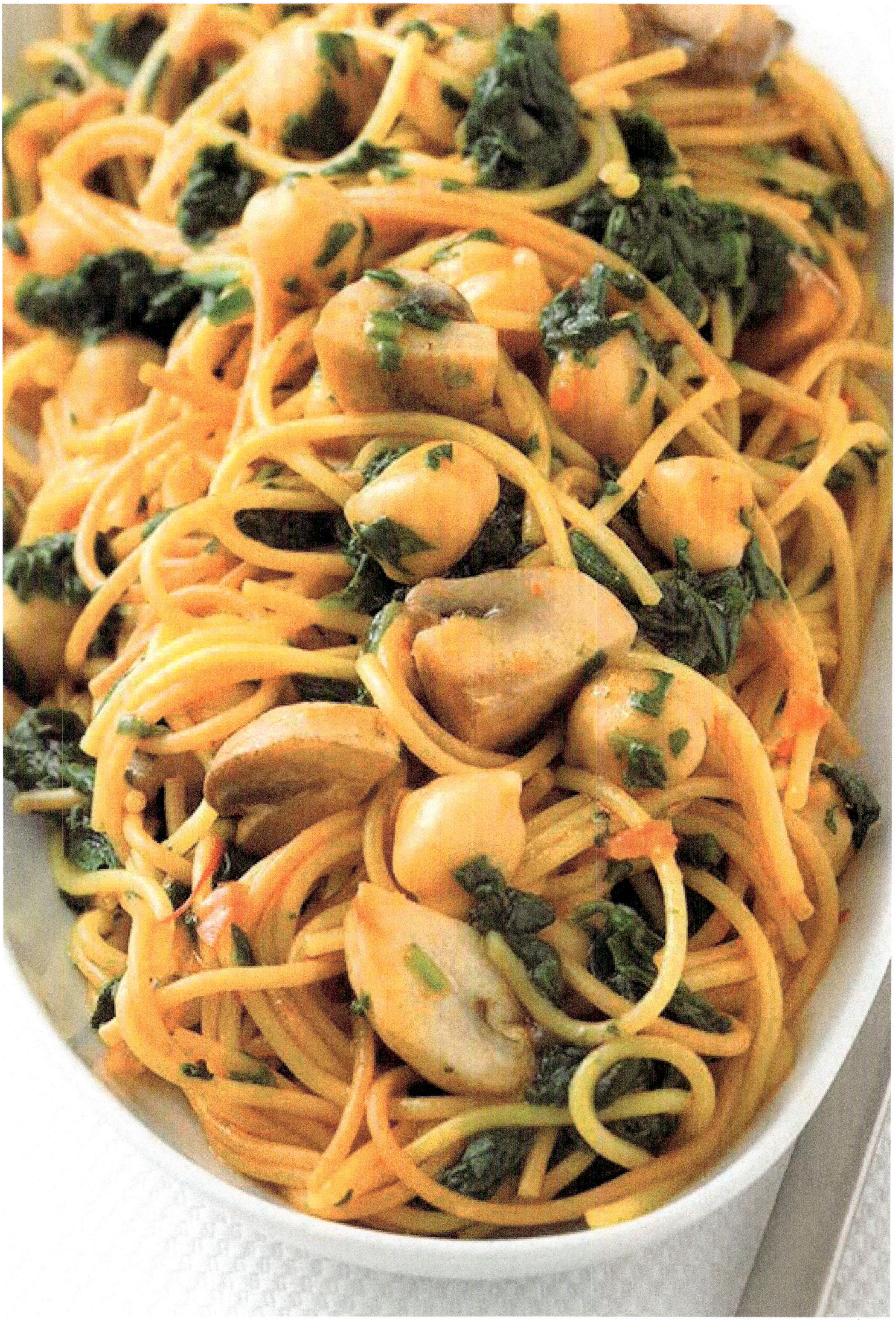

Table of Contents

Introduction	**1**
Chapter 1	
Basics of Diabetes	**2**
The Types of Diabetes	3
What is Diabetes and the Diabetic Diet	3
The Main Goals and Benefits of a Diabetic Diet	4
Understanding Carbohydrates and Blood Sugar	4
Chapter 2	
Planning a Diabetic Diet	**6**
Meal Planning for Diabetics	7
Components of a Balanced Diabetic Diet	7
Portion Sizes and Controlling Calories	7
Chapter 3	
Managing Diabetes Through Diet	**8**
How to Monitor Blood Sugar Levels	9
Special Occasions and Eating Out	9
Developing a Personalized Plan with your Healthcare Provider	10
Chapter 4	
30 Days Meal Plan	**11**
Chapter 5	
Breakfast	**14**
Spiced Seeds and Nuts Granola	15
Lemon-Blueberry Overnight Oats	15
Berry-French Toast Stratas	16
Chocolate Pancakes with Strawberries	16
Banana Cauliflower Smoothie	16
Raspberry Choco Oatmeal	17
Strawberry and Ricotta Pancakes	17
Apple Cinnamon Chia Pudding	18
Bell Peppered Rings with Egg & Avocado Salsa	18
Whole-Grain Strawberry Pancakes	19
Breakfast Pizza	19
Cafe Mocha Smoothies	20
Blueberry Cinnamon Muffins	20
Blueberry English Muffin Loaf	21
Veggie Fillets Omelets	21
Blueberry Stuffed French Toast	22
Cauliflower Breakfast Hash	22
Chapter 6	
Soups, Salads, and Stews	**23**
Curried Carrot Soup	24
Thai Peanut, Carrot, and Shourimp Soup	24
Chicken Tortilla Soup	24
Meatball Vegetable Stew	25
Lentil Potato Stew	25
Tofu Soup	25
Bacon Vegetable Stew	25
Bean Soup (Tuscan Style)	25
Cheesy Chicken Tortilla Soup	26

Taco Soup	26
Beef, Mushouroom, and Pearl Barley Soup	26
Lamb and Vegetable Stew	27
Leek and Cauliflower Soup	27
French Onion Gruyere Soup	27
Chicken Zucchini Noodle Soup	27
Chicken Coconut Soup	28
Cucumber, Tomato, and Avocado Salad	28
Cabbage Slaw Salad	28
Chicken Noodle Soup	29
Golden Soup	29
Spring Vegetable Soup	29

Chapter 7
Chicken and Poultry — 30

Chicken Loaf	31
Peanut Chicken Satay	31
Onion Fried Chicken	31
Chicken Tuscany	31
Chicken Pappardelle	32
Stuffed Chicken Breasts	32
Chicken Salad	32
Chicken Stuffed with Mushourooms	33
Chicken Stew	33
Chicken Marsala	33
Turkey and Avocado Patties	33
Chicken Zucchini Patties with Salsa	34
Easy Chicken Cacciatore	34
Chicken Salad with Fruits	34
Chicken & Spinach Pasta Skillet	35
Roasted Chicken with Root Vegetables	35
Coconut Crusted Chicken Tenders	35
Lettuce Salad with Turkey	36
Spatchcock with Lime Aioli	36
Carrots and Kale with Chicken	36
Ritzy Jerked Chicken Breasts	37
Roasted Vegetable and Chicken Tortillas	37

Chapter 8
Beef, Lamb and Pork — 38

Bunless Sloppy Joes	39
Easy Beef Curry	39
Asian-Style Grilled Beef Salad	39
Barbecue Pork Loin	40
Corned Beef and Cabbage Soup with Barley	40
Korean-Inspired Beef	41
Orange-Marinated Pork Tenderloin	41
Mushouroom Sauced Pork Chops	42
Raspberry Lemon Glazed Pork Chops	42
Homestyle Herb Meatballs	42
Pulled Pork Loin	43
Pork and Cabbage Stir-Fry	43
Sloppy Joes	43
Roasted Spice-Rubbed Pork Tenderloin	44
Mediterranean Lamb Bowl	44
Mediterranean Pork Chops	44

Chapter 9
Fish and Seafood — 45

Baked Salmon with Garlic Parmesan Topping	46
Salmon Mozzarella Salad	46
BBQ Oysters with Bacon	46
Cajun Catfish	46
Salmon Zucchini Salad	47
Ginger-Glazed Salmon and Broccoli	47
Blackened Shourimp	47
Cajun Flounder & Tomatoes	47
Roasted Salmon with Salsa Verde	48
Ceviche	48
Baked Seafood Casserole	49
Ahi Poke and Avocado Salad Served with Macadamia Nuts	49
Salmon Avocado Salad	49

Chapter 10
Vegetable and Side Dishes — 50

Veggie Fajitas with Guacamole	51
Chimichurri Dumplings	51
Redux Okra Callaloo	51
Baby Spinach minutesi Quiches	52
Spaghetti Squash and Chickpea Bolognese	52
Black Bean Enchilada Skillet Casserole	52
Not Slow-Cooked Collards	53
Garlic Onion and Tomato	53
Spicy Mustard Greens	53
Mushouroom and Cauliflower Rice Risotto	53
Beet, Goat Cheese, and Walnut Pesto with Zoodles	54
Cauli-Flowing Sweet Potato	54
Mushouroom and Pesto Flatbread Pizza	54
One Pot Hot Corn	54
Lemony Broccoli	55
Butter Yams	55

Chapter 11
Snacks and Desserts — 56

Chai Pear-Fig Compote	57
Peanut Butter Protein Bites	57
Vanilla Bean N'Ice Cream	57
Lemon Dessert Shots	57
Pomegranate-Tequila Sunrise Jelly Shots	58
Almond Cheesecake Bites	58
Snickers Bar	58
Black Bottom Pie	59
Almond Coconut Biscotti	59
Mixed-Berry Snack Cake	60
Garlic Kale Chips	60
Asian Chicken Wings	60
Sugar-Free Cake	60
Chocolate Chip Cookies	61
Almond Flour Crackers	61
Banana Nut Cookies	61
BLT Stuffed Cucumbers	61

Appendix 1 Measurement Conversion Chart — 62
Appendix 2 The Dirty Dozen and Clean Fifteen — 63
Appendix 3 Index — 64

Introduction

Reducing sugar and simple carbs is part of an exhaustive weight-loss management strategy for most people. However, for those who have diabetes, this basic strategy can be about life or death.

People with diabetes are up to four times more likely to die of heart disease and stroke. The odds of numerous health issues increase exponentially for those who do not manage the condition. It is the reason why this cookbook was necessary.

It contains recipes and tips for all types of meals. Whether for breakfast, supper, or snacks, you will find healthy recipes to help you to manage the condition. Proper food intake can help strengthen the body, making it more resilient to conditions that could lower your quality of life.

Chapter 1
Basics of Diabetes

The Types of Diabetes

Knowledge of diabetes is lacking for most people. It is only after a diagnosis that they begin to understand the condition. Diabetes can be either type 1 or type 2.

Type 1 diabetes is an autoimmune condition that is managed using insulin. It is present from childhood for a majority of people.

Type 2 diabetes is the most prevalent and is classified as a lifestyle disease. It mainly affects obese people in their 40s or higher. In most cases, it can be managed with exercise and a healthy diet. Depending on the severity of the condition, medication is sometimes needed.

People with Type 2 diabetes do not need to change their diet drastically. However, they must have snacks and meals throughout the day. With some basic tips, eating healthy can be a breeze. This cookbook was created with these considerations in mind.

What is Diabetes and the Diabetic Diet

Diabetes is a chronic condition in which the body is unable to properly regulate blood sugar levels. There are two main types of diabetes: type 1 and type 2. In type 1 diabetes, the body is unable to produce enough insulin, which is a hormone that helps regulate blood sugar levels. In type 2 diabetes, the body is unable to properly use the insulin that it produces.

Managing diabetes through diet involves eating a balanced and healthy diet, and monitoring your intake of carbohydrates, which can affect blood sugar levels. This may involve following a specific meal plan and monitoring your portions, as well as making sure to include a variety of fruits, vegetables, and whole grains in your diet. It is also important to limit your intake of processed and sugary foods, and to avoid skipping meals. In some cases, medication may also be necessary to help manage blood sugar levels.

THE IMPORTANCE OF THE DIABETIC DIET

Following a healthy and balanced diabetic diet is important for several reasons. First, it can help control blood sugar levels and prevent them from becoming too high or too low. This can help prevent complications such as heart disease, nerve damage, and kidney damage, which are common in people with diabetes.

A healthy and balanced diabetic diet can also help maintain a healthy weight, which is important for managing diabetes and reducing the risk of other health conditions. Eating a variety of healthy foods can also provide the vitamins, minerals, and other nutrients that the body needs to function properly.

Additionally, following a healthy and balanced diabetic diet can help reduce the risk of other chronic conditions, such as heart disease and high blood pressure, which are common in people with diabetes. By eating a diet that is rich in fruits, vegetables, whole grains, and lean proteins, and low in processed and sugary foods, people with diabetes can help support their overall health and wellbeing.

The Main Goals and Benefits of a Diabetic Diet

The main goals and benefits of a diabetic diet are:

To control blood sugar levels and prevent them from becoming too high or too low. This can help prevent complications such as heart disease, nerve damage, and kidney damage, which are common in people with diabetes.

To maintain a healthy weight. Being overweight or obese can increase the risk of developing diabetes and can make it more difficult to manage the condition. A healthy diet can help people with diabetes maintain a healthy weight and reduce the risk of other health conditions.

To provide the body with the vitamins, minerals, and other nutrients it needs to function properly. A healthy and balanced diabetic diet can help ensure that the body gets the nutrients it needs to support overall health and wellbeing.

To reduce the risk of other chronic conditions. Eating a diet that is rich in fruits, vegetables, whole grains, and lean proteins, and low in processed and sugary foods, can help reduce the risk of other chronic conditions, such as heart disease and high blood pressure, which are common in people with diabetes.

To support overall health and wellbeing. By following a healthy and balanced diabetic diet, people with diabetes can support their overall health and wellbeing, and improve their quality of life.

Understanding Carbohydrates and Blood Sugar

HOW CARBOHYDRATES AFFECT BLOOD SUGAR LEVELS

Carbohydrates are a type of macronutrient that the body uses for energy. When we eat carbohydrates, they are broken down into sugar (glucose) in the body, which then enters the bloodstream. The hormone insulin, which is produced by the pancreas, helps to regulate blood sugar levels by allowing the sugar to enter the body's cells, where it is used for energy.

When we eat too many carbohydrates, or foods that are high in refined carbohydrates, such as sugary drinks, candy, and processed snacks, our blood sugar levels can rise quickly. This can be harmful for people with diabetes, as high blood sugar levels can damage the body's cells and tissues over time.

On the other hand, when we eat fewer carbohydrates, or foods that are high in complex carbohydrates, such as fruits, vegetables, and whole grains, our blood sugar levels can rise more slowly, which is healthier for people with diabetes. By monitoring and controlling their intake of carbohydrates, people with diabetes can help manage their blood sugar levels and reduce their risk of complications.

DIFFERENT TYPES OF CARBOHYDRATES

There are two main types of carbohydrates: simple carbohydrates and complex carbohydrates.

Simple carbohydrates are found in foods that are high in sugar, such as candy, cookies, and sugary drinks. They are also found in fruits, vegetables, and dairy products. Simple carbohydrates are quickly broken down by the body and can cause a rapid rise in blood sugar levels.

Complex carbohydrates are found in foods that are high in fiber, such as fruits, vegetables, whole grains, and legumes. They are broken down more slowly by the body, which can help prevent a rapid rise in blood sugar levels.

In general, it is recommended that people with diabetes focus on eating complex carbohydrates, and limit their intake of simple carbohydrates. This can help regulate blood sugar levels and reduce the risk of complications. However, it is also important to monitor overall carbohydrate intake and to follow a healthy and balanced diet.

BALANCING CARBOHYDRATES WITH MEDICATION AND PHYSICAL ACTIVITY

Balancing carbohydrates with medication and physical activity is important for people with diabetes because it can help regulate blood sugar levels and prevent them from becoming too high or too low. When blood sugar levels are not properly controlled, it can lead to complications such as heart disease, nerve damage, and kidney damage.

Eating a balanced diet that includes a variety of fruits, vegetables, and whole grains can help regulate blood sugar levels. However, in some cases, medication may also be necessary to help manage blood sugar levels. For example, insulin injections or oral medications can help the body use or produce insulin more effectively, which can help regulate blood sugar levels.

In addition to medication and diet, physical activity is also important for people with diabetes. Regular exercise can help the body use insulin more efficiently and can also help lower blood sugar levels. It is recommended that people with diabetes get at least 150 minutes of moderate-intensity physical activity per week.

By balancing carbohydrates with medication and physical activity, people with diabetes can help manage their blood sugar levels and reduce their risk of complications.

Chapter 2
Planning a Diabetic Diet

Meal Planning for Diabetics

Meal planning is an important part of managing diabetes because it helps to regulate blood sugar levels. When people with diabetes eat meals that are high in carbohydrates, their blood sugar levels can rise quickly. This can lead to a condition called hyperglycemia, which can have serious health consequences if left untreated. By planning meals in advance, people with diabetes can ensure that they are eating balanced, healthy meals that will help to keep their blood sugar levels within a healthy range. This can help to prevent complications from diabetes and improve overall health.

Components of a Balanced Diabetic Diet

A balanced diabetic diet typically includes a variety of fruits and vegetables, whole grains, lean proteins, and healthy fats. Fruits and vegetables are an important part of a diabetic diet because they are rich in vitamins, minerals, and fiber, and can help regulate blood sugar levels. Whole grains, such as whole wheat bread, brown rice, and oatmeal, are also an important part of a diabetic diet because they provide complex carbohydrates, which can help regulate blood sugar levels and provide long-lasting energy. Lean proteins, such as chicken, fish, and tofu, are also an important part of a diabetic diet because they provide essential nutrients, such as iron and B vitamins, and can help regulate blood sugar levels. Healthy fats, such as olive oil, avocado, and nuts, are also an important part of a diabetic diet because they provide essential fatty acids and can help regulate blood sugar levels.

Portion Sizes and Controlling Calories

Portion sizes and calorie control are important for weight management because they can help people maintain a healthy weight. Portion sizes refer to the amount of food that is consumed at one time, and controlling portion sizes can help people avoid consuming too many calories. Consuming too many calories can lead to weight gain, which can increase the risk of developing health problems such as diabetes, heart disease, and high blood pressure.

Calorie control, on the other hand, refers to the total number of calories that a person consumes each day. Consuming too many calories can lead to weight gain, while consuming too few calories can lead to weight loss. However, it is important to consume the right amount of calories to maintain a healthy weight. This can be achieved by eating a balanced diet that includes a variety of fruits and vegetables, whole grains, lean proteins, and healthy fats. It is also important to engage in regular physical activity, which can help burn calories and support weight management.

Tips for Better Meals

These tips can help you if you have a diabetes diagnosis. Here are some of them:

ADD FLAVOR TO EVERY MEAL

Eliminating sugar and salt from your diet does not mean you have to eat bland, cardboard-like meals. Instead of focusing on what you have cut out, find new ways to flavor meals. There are numerous ways to do this without salt or sugar. One option is to use fresh herbs, ginger, garlic, and pepper. Make it your mission to experiment with as many spices as possible.

ADD PROTEINS TO YOUR DIET

Proteins from high-quality sources, like fish, help to stabilize blood sugar. Besides that, they keep you feeling full for longer. Lean protein should be added to every meal. Some options for lean protein are hummus, nuts, beans, turkey, pork tenderloin, and tuna. While animal proteins contain little to no carbs, legumes could have some carbs. As such, read labels carefully not to exceed your carb intake.

EAT OFTEN

When you receive a diabetes diagnosis, the first step is to lose weight. It can be tempting to skip meals. However, it does not work; doing so could actually trigger a mechanism that causes your body to gain weight. Instead, have a meal at least every five hours.

Chapter 3
Managing Diabetes Through Diet

Meal timing and consistency are important for managing diabetes because they can help regulate blood sugar levels. Eating balanced meals at regular intervals can help prevent large fluctuations in blood sugar levels, which can be harmful for people with diabetes. Consuming meals and snacks at regular intervals throughout the day can help maintain stable blood sugar levels, which can prevent the onset of diabetes-related complications such as heart disease, nerve damage, and kidney damage.

In addition to regular meal times, it is also important for people with diabetes to be consistent in their eating habits. This means eating similar types and amounts of foods at each meal, and avoiding skipping meals or making large changes to their diet. Consistency in eating habits can help regulate blood sugar levels and make it easier for people with diabetes to manage their condition.

Overall, meal timing and consistency are important for managing diabetes because they can help regulate blood sugar levels and prevent the onset of diabetes-related complications.

How to Monitor Blood Sugar Levels

To monitor blood sugar levels and adjust medication and diet accordingly, people with diabetes should regularly test their blood sugar levels using a blood glucose meter. This device measures the amount of glucose, or sugar, in the blood and provides a numerical reading. The American Diabetes Association recommends that people with diabetes test their blood sugar levels at least once a day, and more frequently if they are taking insulin or other medications that can affect blood sugar levels.

Once a person has tested their blood sugar level, they can adjust their medication and diet accordingly. If the blood sugar level is too high, they may need to take additional medication, such as insulin, to bring it down to a healthy level. They may also need to adjust their diet by reducing their intake of carbohydrates and increasing their intake of protein and healthy fats.

Conversely, if the blood sugar level is too low, they may need to take steps to raise it to a healthy level. This can include eating a snack that contains carbohydrates, such as fruit or crackers, or taking glucose tablets. They may also need to adjust their medication and diet to prevent future episodes of low blood sugar.

Overall, monitoring blood sugar levels and adjusting medication and diet accordingly is an important part of managing diabetes and preventing complications.

Special Occasions and Eating Out

When following a diabetic diet, it is important to be mindful of what you eat on special occasions and when eating out. Here are some tips for handling these situations:

Plan ahead: Before attending a special event or eating out, take a few minutes to review the menu and plan what you will eat. Look for dishes that are low in sugar, fat, and calories, and that are high in protein, fiber, and complex carbohydrates.

Make smart substitutions: When ordering, ask for substitutions to make the dish healthier. For example, ask for steamed vegetables instead of french fries, or for grilled chicken instead of fried chicken.

Watch your portion sizes: It can be tempting to overindulge on special occasions, but it is important to control your portion sizes to avoid consuming too many calories. Use a smaller plate to help control portion sizes, and avoid going back for seconds.

Choose your drinks wisely: Alcoholic beverages and sugary drinks can be high in calories and can spike blood sugar levels. Choose low-calorie and sugar-free options, and limit your intake of alcohol to avoid overconsumption.

Don't skip meals: Skipping meals can lead to low blood sugar levels, which can be dangerous for people with diabetes. Be sure to eat regular, balanced meals, even on special occasions and when eating out.

Overall, it is important for people with diabetes to be mindful of what they eat on special occasions and when eating out. By planning ahead, making smart substitutions, watching portion sizes, choosing drinks wisely, and avoiding skipping meals, people with diabetes can enjoy special occasions and eating out while still following a healthy, balanced diet.

Developing a Personalized Plan with your Healthcare Provider

If you have diabetes, it is important to work with a healthcare provider to develop a personalized plan for managing your condition through diet. A healthcare provider can help you understand your specific nutritional needs and create a plan that is tailored to your individual circumstances. They can also provide guidance and support on topics such as meal planning, portion sizes, and food choices, and can help you make changes to your diet in a safe and effective way.

Additionally, a healthcare provider can monitor your progress and make adjustments to your plan as needed. They can also help you manage any complications that may arise, such as high or low blood sugar levels, and can provide support and resources to help you stay on track.

Working with a healthcare provider is an important step in managing your diabetes through diet, and can help ensure that you are following a plan that is safe and effective for your individual needs. So, if you have diabetes, be sure to talk to your healthcare provider about developing a personalized plan for managing your condition through diet.

SUMMARY

In this cookbook, you will find detailed recipes to eat healthy with diabetes. They are all designed to be visually pleasing, nutritious, and tasty.

Try them today!

Chapter 4
30 Days Meal Plan

Days	Breakfast	Lunch	Dinner
Day 1	Spiced Seeds and Nuts Granola	Meatball Vegetable Stew	Peanut Chicken Satay
Day 2	Banana Cauliflower Smoothie	Salmon Mozzarella Salad	Redux Okra Callaloo
Day 3	Chocolate Pancakes with Strawberries	Easy Beef Curry	Ceviche
Day 4	Lemon-Blueberry Overnight Oats	Chimichurri Dumplings	Lentil Potato Stew
Day 5	Raspberry Choco Oatmeal	Korean-Inspired Beef	Baby Spinach minutesi Quiches
Day 6	Strawberry and Ricotta Pancakes	Salmon Zucchini Salad	Black Bean Enchilada Skillet Casserole
Day 7	Berry-French Toast Stratas	One Pot Hot Corn	Garlic Onion and Tomato
Day 8	Whole-Grain Strawberry Pancakes	Barbecue Pork Loin	Spicy Mustard Greens
Day 9	Chocolate Pancakes with Strawberries	Onion Fried Chicken	Chimichurri Dumplings
Day 10	Breakfast Pizza	Lemony Broccoli	Mediterranean Lamb Bowl
Day 11	Blueberry Cinnamon Muffins	Asian-Style Grilled Beef Salad	Butter Yams
Day 12	Blueberry English Muffin Loaf	Blackened Shourimp	Chicken Tuscany
Day 13	Lemon-Blueberry Overnight Oats	Pulled Pork Loin	Golden Soup
Day 14		Homestyle Herb Meatballs	Cabbage Slaw Salad

Day 15	Raspberry Choco Oatmeal	Tofu Soup	Cajun Catfish
Day 16	Veggie Fillets Omelets	Chicken Loaf	Chicken Noodle Soup
Day 17	Blueberry Stuffed French Toast	Sloppy Joes	Cucumber, Tomato, and Avocado Salad
Day 18	Cauliflower Breakfast Hash	Chicken Pappardelle	Taco Soup
Day 19	Spiced Seeds and Nuts Granola	Mushouroom Sauced Pork Chops	Leek and Cauliflower Soup
Day 20	Sugar-Free Cake	BBQ Oysters with Bacon	Lamb and Vegetable Stew
Day 21	Cafe Mocha Smoothies	Bacon Vegetable Stew	Pulled Pork Loin
Day 22	Lemon-Blueberry Overnight Oats	Chicken Noodle Soup	Chicken Marsala
Day 23	Apple Cinnamon Chia Pudding	Salmon Mozzarella Salad	Bean Soup (Tuscan Style)
Day 24	Sugar-Free Cake	Corned Beef and Cabbage Soup with Barley	Black Bean Enchilada Skillet Casserole
Day 25	Berry-French Toast Stratas	Ceviche	Meatball Vegetable Stew
Day 26	Blueberry English Muffin Loaf	Peanut Chicken Satay	Spaghetti Squash and Chickpea Bolognese
Day 27	Blueberry Cinnamon Muffins	Chicken Marsala	Not Slow-Cooked Collards
Day 28	Spiced Seeds and Nuts Granola	Turkey and Avocado Patties	Bean Soup (Tuscan Style)
Day 29	Strawberry and Ricotta Pancakes	Chicken Salad with Fruits	Mushouroom and Cauliflower Rice Risotto
Day 30	Breakfast Pizza	Blackened Shourimp	Ginger-Glazed Salmon and Broccoli

Chapter 5
Breakfast

Spiced Seeds and Nuts Granola

Prep time: 5 minutes | Cook time: 25 minutes | Serves 8

- 2 cups gluten-free rolled oats
- ½ cup raw sunflower seeds
- ½ cup shouredded unsweetened coconut
- ½ cup chopped pecans
- ½ cup slivered almonds
- ¼ cup maple syrup
- 2 tablespoons canola oil
- ½ teaspoon ground cinnamon
- ¼ teaspoon ground nutmeg
- ⅛ teaspoon sea salt

1. Preheat the oven to 300°F and line a baking sheet with parchment paper. Set it aside.
2. In a large bowl, toss together the oats, sunflower seeds, coconut, pecans, and almonds until mixed.
3. In a small bowl, whisk the maple syrup, oil, cinnamon, nutmeg, and salt until blended.
4. Add the maple syrup mixture to the oat mixture and mix until very well coated.
5. Spread the oat mixture on the baking sheet and bake for about 25 minutes, stirring frequently, until the granola is golden brown and crunchy.
6. Let the granola cool, break up the large pieces, and store in an airtight container in the refrigerator or freezer for up to 1 month.

PER SERVING

Calories 289| Cook fat 18g| Saturated fat 3g| Sodium 43mg| Carbohydrates 25g| Sugar 7g| Fiber 5g| Protein 7g

Lemon-Blueberry Overnight Oats

Prep time: 5 minutes, plus sitting overnight | Serves 2

- ½ cup milk of choice
- ½ cup low-fat plain Greek yogurt
- ½ cup gluten-free rolled oats
- 2 tablespoons chia seeds
- Juice and zest of 1 lemon
- 1 tablespoon maple syrup
- 1 teaspoon pure vanilla extract
- Pinch sea salt
- 1 cup blueberries

1. In a medium bowl, whisk the milk, yogurt, oats, chia seeds, lemon juice, lemon zest, maple syrup, vanilla, and salt.
2. Fold in the blueberries, cover, and refrigerate for at least 4 hours or overnight.

PER SERVING

Calories 283| Cook fat 6g| Saturated fat 1g| Sodium 133mg| Carbohydrates 42g| Sugar 17g| Fiber 10g| Protein 10g

Berry-French Toast Stratas

Prep time: 15 minutes | Cook time: 50 minutes | Serves 6

- 3 cups assorted fresh berries, such as blueberries, raspberries or cut-up strawberries
- 1 tablespoon granulated sugar
- 4 cups cubes (3/4 inch) whole wheat bread (about 5 slices)
- 1 1/2 cups fat-free egg product or 6 eggs
- 1/2 cup fat-free (skim) milk
- 1/2 cup fat-free half-and-half
- 2 tablespoons honey
- 1 1/2 teaspoons vanilla
- 1 teaspoon ground cinnamon
- 1/4 teaspoon ground nutmeg
- 1/2 teaspoon powdered sugar, if desired

1. In medium bowl, mix fruit and granulated sugar; set aside.
2. Heat oven to 350°F.
3. Spray 12 regular-size muffin cups generously with Cook spray.
4. Divide bread cubes evenly among muffin cups.
5. In large bowl, beat remaining ingredients, except powdered sugar, with fork or whisk until well mixed.
6. Pour egg mixture over bread cubes, pushing down lightly with spoon to soak bread cubes. (If all egg mixture doesn't fit into cups, let cups stand up to 10 minutes, gradually adding remaining egg mixture as bread cubes soak it up.)
7. Bake 20 to 25 minutes or until centers are set. Cool 5 minutes.
8. Remove from muffin cups, placing 2 stratas on each of 6 plates.
9. Divide fruit mixture evenly over stratas; sprinkle with powdered sugar.

PER SERVING

Calories 190 (Calories from Fat 15)| Cook Fat 1.5g (Saturated Fat 0g| Trans Fat 0g)| Cholesterol 0mg| Sodium 280mg| Cook Carbohydrate 31g |Dietary Fiber 5g| Sugars 18g| Protein 11g

Chocolate Pancakes with Strawberries

Prep time: 25 minutes|Cook time: 25 minutes | Serves 4

- 3/4 cup light chocolate soymilk
- 1/4 cup fat-free egg product
- 1 tablespoon canola oil
- 3/4 cup all-purpose flour
- 2 tablespoons sugar
- 2 tablespoons unsweetened baking cocoa
- 1 teaspoon baking powder
- 1/8 teaspoon salt
- 1 cup sliced fresh strawberries
- Sliced banana, if desired
- French vanilla fat-free yogurt, if desired

1. In medium bowl, beat soymilk, egg product and oil with whisk until smooth.
2. Stir in remaining ingredients except strawberries, banana and yogurt.
3. Spray griddle or 10-inch skillet with Cook spray; heat griddle to 375°F or heat skillet over medium heat.
4. For each pancake, pour slightly less than 1/4 cup batter onto hot griddle.
5. Cook pancakes until puffed and dry around edges.
6. Turn and Cook other sides until golden brown.
7. Serve with strawberries, banana and yogurt.

PER SERVING

Calories 210 (Calories from Fat 45)| Cook Fat 4.5g (Saturated Fat 0g| Trans Fat 0g)| Cholesterol 0mg| Sodium 260mg| Cook Carbohydrate 36g |Dietary Fiber 3g| Sugars 11g| Protein 6g

Banana Cauliflower Smoothie

Prep time: 5 minutes | Cook time: 10 minutes | Serves 1

- 2 cups of unsweetened plain almond milk
- 2 teaspoons of maple syrup
- 1 cup of frozen riced cauliflower
- 1/2 cup of frozen mixed berries
- 1 cup of sliced frozen banana

1. Place cauliflower, banana, berries, maple syrup, and almond milk in a blender.
2. Blend for about 3 to 4 minutes until smooth.

PER SERVING

Calories 149|Protein 3g|Carbohydrates 21.3g|Dietary fiber 5g|Sugars 14.5g| Fat 3g| Calcium 473.6mg| Sodium 184.4mg| Added sugar 4g

Raspberry Choco Oatmeal

Prep time: 10 minutes | Cook time: 20 minutes | Serves 4

- 3 cups of unsweetened almond milk
- 1 cup of fresh red raspberries
- 1-1/2 cups of regular rolled oats
- 2 tablespoons of unsweetened cocoa powder
- 1/4 teaspoon of salt
- 4 teaspoons of sugar-free chocolate-flavor syrup (Optional)

1. Mix the salt, oats, and cocoa powder in a saucepan.
2. Add the almonds and milk.
3. Bring to a boil over medium heat, stirring occasionally.
4. Lower the heat and simmer until thick, about 5 to 7 minutes, stirring.
5. Cover and remove from heat.
6. Allow resting for about 3 minutes.
7. Divide the oatmeal mixture among 4 bowls.
8. Top each serving with about 1/4 cup raspberries.
9. On top of each serving, sprinkle with 1 teaspoon of chocolate syrup (to taste). Serve and enjoy!

PER SERVING

Calories 157| Protein 5.4g| Carbohydrates 26.2g| Dietary fiber 6.6g| Sugars 2.2g| Fat 4.7g| Calcium 348.7mg

Strawberry and Ricotta Pancakes

Prep time: 10 minutes | Cook time: 20 minutes | Serves 4

- 1¼ cups milk of choice
- ½ cup low-fat ricotta cheese
- 1 large egg
- 1 tablespoon canola oil
- 1 tablespoon freshly squeezed lemon juice
- ½ teaspoon pure vanilla extract
- 1¼ cups whole-wheat flour
- 1 tablespoon sugar
- 2 teaspoons baking powder
- ¼ teaspoon salt
- Canola oil, for Cook
- 1 cup sliced strawberries

1. In a large bowl, whisk the milk, ricotta, egg, oil, lemon juice, and vanilla until well blended.
2. Whisk in the flour, sugar, baking powder, and salt until combined.
3. Heat a griddle or large skillet on medium heat and lightly grease it with oil.
4. Reduce the heat to medium-low and, working in batches, add the batter in ¼-cup measures.
5. Cook until the edges of the pancakes are firm and golden, about 2 minutes, then scatter the strawberries on top of each, and flip.
6. Cook the pancakes for 1 minutesute more until Cooked thourough, transfer them to a plate, and cover loosely with aluminutesum foil to keep them warm.
7. Repeat with the remaining batter and serve.

PER SERVING

Calories 285| Cook fat 9g| Saturated fat 2g| Sodium 220mg| Carbohydrates 40g| Sugar: 9g| Fiber 5g| Protein 12g

Apple Cinnamon Chia Pudding

Prep time: 10 minutes | Cook time: 8 hours 10 minutes | Serves 1

- 1/4 teaspoon of vanilla extract
- 1/4 teaspoon of ground cinnamon
- 1/2 cup of diced apple, divided
- 1/2 cup of unsweetened almond milk or other nondairy milk
- 2 tablespoons of chia seeds
- 2 teaspoons of pure maple syrup
- 1 tablespoon of chopped toasted pecans, divided

1. In a small bowl, stir chia, almond milk (or other non-dairy milk), maple syrup, chia, cinnamon, and vanilla.
2. Cover and refrigerate for about 8 hours and up to 3 days.
3. Stir well when ready to serve.
4. Spoon about half of the pudding into a serving bowl or glass.
5. Top with half the pecans and apple.
6. Add the rest of the pudding.
7. Top with the rest of the pecans and apples.
8. Serve and enjoy!

PER SERVING

Calories 233| Protein 4.8g| Carbohydrates 27.7g| Dietary fiber 10.1g| Sugars 14.4g| Fat 12.7g| Calcium 385.9mg

Bell Peppered Rings with Egg & Avocado Salsa

Prep time: 20 minutes | Cook time: 1 hour | Serves 12

- 2 tomatoes, seeded and diced
- Juice of 1 lime
- 3/4 teaspoon of salt, divided
- 2 teaspoons of olive oil, divided
- 8 large eggs
- 2 bell peppers of any color
- 1 avocado, diced
- 1/2 cup of diced red onion
- 1 jalapeño pepper, minutesced
- 1/2 cup of chopped fresh cilantro, plus more for garnish
- 1/4 teaspoon of ground pepper, divided

1. Slice the bottoms and tops off bell peppers, then finely dice.
2. Remove and discard membranes and seeds.
3. Slice each pepper into four half-inch thick rings.
4. Combine the diced pepper with onion, avocado, cilantro, jalapeno, lime juice, tomatoes, and half a teaspoon of salt in a medium bowl.
5. In a large nonstick skillet, heat about 1 teaspoon of oil over medium heat.
6. Add 4 bell pepper rings, then crack about 1 egg into the middle of each ring.
7. Season with 1/8 teaspoon of each pepper and salt.
8. Cook for about 2 to 3 minutes until the whites are mostly set but yolks are still runny.
9. Flip gently and Cook for about a minutesute more for runny yolks. Transfer into serving plates.
10. Repeat with the rest of the pepper rings and eggs.
11. Serve and enjoy!

PER SERVING

Calories 285| Protein 15.1g| Carbohydrates 14.2g| Dietary fiber 5.9g| Sugars 5.9g| Fat 19.5g| Calcium 81.2mg

Whole-Grain Strawberry Pancakes

Prep time: 30 minutes | Cook time: 30 minutes | Serves 7

- 1 1/2 cups whole wheat flour
- 3 tablespoons sugar
- 1 teaspoon baking powder
- 1/2 teaspoon baking soda
- 1/2 teaspoon salt
- 3 eggs or 3/4 cup fat-free egg product
- 1 container (6 oz) vanilla low-fat yogurt
- 3/4 cup water
- 3 tablespoons canola oil
- 1 3/4 cups sliced fresh strawberries
- 1 container (6 oz) strawberry low-fat yogurt

1. Heat griddle to 375°F or heat 12-inch skillet over medium heat.
2. Grease with canola oil if necessary (or spray with Cook spray before heating).
3. In large bowl, mix flour, sugar, baking powder, baking soda and salt; set aside.
4. In medium bowl, beat eggs, vanilla yogurt, water and oil with egg beater or whisk until well blended.
5. Pour egg mixture all at once into flour mixture; stir until moistened.
6. For each pancake, pour slightly less than 1/4 cup batter onto hot griddle. Cook pancakes 1 to 2 minutes or until bubbly on top, puffed and dry around edges. Turn; Cook other sides 1 to 2 minutes or until golden brown.
7. Top each serving with 1/4 cup sliced strawberries and 1 to 2 tablespoons strawberry yogurt.

PER SERVING

Calories 260 (Calories from Fat 90)| Cook Fat 9g (Saturated Fat 1.5g| Trans Fat 0g)| Cholesterol 95mg| Sodium 380mg| Cook Carbohydrate 34g (Dietary Fiber 4g| Sugars 13g)| Protein 8g

Breakfast Pizza

Prep time: 10 minutes | Cook time: 30 minutes | Serves 8

- 12 eggs
- 1/2 lb. breakfast sausage
- 1 cup bell pepper, sliced
- 1 cup red pepper, sliced
- 1 cup cheddar cheese, grated
- 1/2 cup half-n-half
- What you'll need from store cupboard:
- 1/2 tsp salt
- 1/4 tsp pepper

1. Heat oven to 350 degrees.
2. In a large cast iron skillet, brown sausage. Transfer to bowl.
3. Add peppers and Cook 3-5 minutes or until they begin to soften. Transfer to a bowl.
4. In a small bowl, whisk together the eggs, cream, salt and pepper. Pour into skillet. Cook 5 minutes or until the sides start to set.
5. Bake 15 minutes.
6. Remove from oven and set it to broil. Top "crust" with sausage, peppers, and cheese. Broil 3 minutes, or until cheese is melted and starts to brown.
7. Let rest 5 minutes before slicing and serving.

PER SERVING

Calories 230| Cook Carbs 4g| Protein 16g| Fat 17g |Sugar 2g |Fiber 0g

The Ultimate Type 2 Diabetes UK Cookbook for Beginners | 19

Cafe Mocha Smoothies
Cook time: 5 minutes| Serves 3

- 1 avocado, remove pit and cut in half
- 1 ½ cup almond milk, unsweetened
- ½ cup canned coconut milk
- What you'll need from store cupboard:
- 3 tbsp. Splenda
- 3 tbsp. unsweetened cocoa powder
- 2 tsp instant coffee
- 1 tsp vanilla

1. Place everything but the avocado in the blender. Process until smooth.
2. Add the avocado and blend until smooth and no chunks remain.
3. Pour into glasses and serve.

PER SERVING

Calories 109 |Cook Carbs 15g |Protein 6g |Fat 1g| Sugar 13g| Fiber 0g

Blueberry Cinnamon Muffins
Prep time: 10 minutes|Cook time: 30 minutes| Serves 10

- 3 eggs
- 1 cup blueberries
- 1/3 cup half-n-half
- ¼ cup margarine, melted
- What you'll need from store cupboard:
- 1½ cup almond flour
- ⅓ cup Splenda
- 1 tsp baking powder
- 1 tsp cinnamon

1. Heat oven to 350 degrees. Line 10 muffin cups with paper liners.
2. In a large mixing bowl, combine dry Ingredients.
3. Stir in wet Ingredients and mix well.
4. Fold in the blueberries and spoon evenly into lined muffin pan.
5. Bake 25-30 minutes or they pass the toothpick test.

PER SERVING

Calories 194|Cook Carbs 12g |Net Carbs 10g |Protein 5g| Fat 14g| Sugar 9g |Fiber 2g

Blueberry English Muffin Loaf
Prep time: 15 minutes | Cook time: 1 hour | Serves 12

- 6 eggs beaten
- ½ cup almond milk, unsweetened
- ½ cup blueberries
- What you'll need from store cupboard:
- ½ cup cashew butter
- ½ cup almond flour
- ¼ cup coconut oil
- 2 tsp baking powder
- ½ tsp salt
- Nonstick Cook spray

1. Heat oven to 350 degrees. Line a loaf pan with parchment paper and spray lightly with Cook spray.
2. In a small glass bowl, melt cashew butter and oil together in the microwave for 30 seconds. Stir until well combined.
3. In a large bowl, stir together the dry Ingredients. Add cashew butter mixture and stir well.
4. In a separate bowl, whisk the milk and eggs together. Add to flour mixture and stir well. Fold in blueberries.
5. Pour into the Prepared pan and bake 45 minutes, or until it passes the toothpick test.
6. Cook 30 minutes, remove from pan and slice.

PER SERVING

Calories 162| Cook Carbs 5g| Net Carbs 4g| Protein 6g| Fat 14g| Sugar 1g |Fiber 1g

Veggie Fillets Omelets
Prep time: 5 minutes | Cook time: 30 minutes | Serves 4

- 1/2 ripe avocado, pitted, peeled, and chopped
- 2 eggs
- 1 cup of refrigerated or frozen egg product,
- 2 tablespoons of water
- 1 snipped fresh chives
- 1 teaspoon of dried basil, crushed
- 1/4 teaspoon of salt
- 1/2 cup of no-salt-added diced tomatoes with garlic, basil, and oregano, well-drained
- 1/2 cup of cucumber, chopped and seeded
- 1/2 cup of chopped yellow summer squash
- 1/4 teaspoon of ground black pepper
- Nonstick Cook spray
- 1/4 cup of shouredded reduced-fat Monterey Jack cheese with jalapeño chile peppers

FOR THE FILLING:
- Mix together the tomatoes, cucumber, squash, and avocado in a bowl and set aside.
- Whisk together the eggs, salt, water, basil, and pepper in a medium bowl.

1. Cook until done for about 30 to 60 seconds.
2. Spoon about 1/2 cup of the filling onto one side of the omelet.
3. Fold the omelet over the filling and remove the omelet from the pan.
4. Repeat to make about 4 omelets Cook, wiping the pan between each omelet.
5. Sprinkle about a tablespoon of cheese over each omelet (to taste). Garnish with chives, then serve and enjoy!

PER SERVING

Calories 128| Protein 12.3g| Carbohydrates 6.7g| Dietary fiber 3.5g| Sugars 4.1g| Fat 6.1g| Calcium 120mg| Sodium 357.5mg

The Ultimate Type 2 Diabetes UK Cookbook for Beginners | 21

Blueberry Stuffed French Toast
Prep time: 15 minutes| Cook time: 20 minutes| Serves 8

- 4 eggs
- 1 ½ cup blueberries
- ½ cup orange juice
- 1 tsp orange zest
- What you'll need from store cupboard:
- 16 slices bread, (chapter 14)
- 3 tbsp. Splenda, divided
- 1/8 tsp salt
- Blueberry Orange Dessert Sauce, (chapter 16)
- Nonstick Cook spray

1. Heat oven to 400 degrees. Spray a large baking sheet with Cook spray.
2. In a small bowl, combine berries with 2 tablespoons of Splenda.
3. Lay 8 slices of bread on work surface. Top with about 3 tablespoons of berries and place second slice of bread on top. Flatten slightly.
4. In a shallow dish, whisk remaining Ingredients together. Carefully dip both sides of bread in egg mixture and place on Prepared pan.
5. Bake 7-12 minutes per side, or until lightly browned.
6. Heat up dessert sauce until warm. Plate the French toast and top with 1-2 tablespoons of the sauce. Serve.

PER SERVING

Calories 208| Cook Carbs 20g |Net Carbs 18g| Protein 7g |Fat 10g |Sugar 14g |Fiber 2g

Cauliflower Breakfast Hash
Prep time: 10 minutes| Cook time: 20 minutes| Serves 2

- 4 cups cauliflower, grated
- 1 cup mushourooms, diced
- ¾ cup onion, diced
- 3 slices bacon
- ¼ cup sharp cheddar cheese, grated

1. In a medium skillet, over med-high heat, fry bacon, set aside.
2. Add vegetables to the skillet and Cook, stirring occasionally, until golden brown.
3. Cut bacon into pieces and return to skillet.
4. Top with cheese and allow it to melt. Serve immediately.

PER SERVING

Calories 155| Cook Carbs 16g| Net Carbs 10g |Protein 10g |Fat 7g |Sugar 7g |Fiber 6g

Chapter 6
Soups, Salads, and Stews

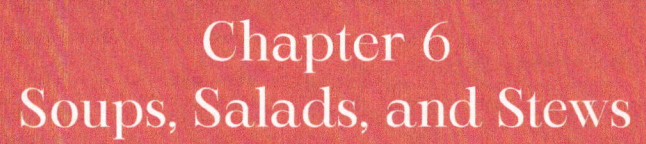

Curried Carrot Soup

Prep time: 10 minutes|Cook time: 5 minutes|Serves 6

- 1 tablespoon extra-virgin olive oil
- 1 small onion, coarsely chopped
- 2 celery stalks, coarsely chopped
- 1½ teaspoons curry powder
- 1 teaspoon ground cuminutes
- 1 teaspoon minutesced fresh ginger
- 6 medium carrots, roughly chopped
- 4 cups low-sodium vegetable broth
- ¼ teaspoon salt
- 1 cup canned coconut milk
- ¼ teaspoon freshly ground black pepper
- 1 tablespoon chopped fresh cilantro

1. Heat an Instant Pot to high and add the olive oil.
2. Sauté the onion and celery for 2 to 3 minutes. Add the curry powder, cuminutes, and ginger to the pot and Cook until fragrant, about 30 seconds.
3. Add the carrots, vegetable broth, and salt to the pot. Close and seal, and set for 5 minutes on high. Allow the pressure to release naturally.
4. In a blender jar, carefully purée the soup in batches and transfer back to the pot.
5. Stir in the coconut milk and pepper, and heat thourough. Top with the cilantro and serve.

PER SERVING

Calories 145| Cook Fat 11g| Protein 2g| Carbohydrates 13g| Sugars 4g| Fiber 3g| Sodium 238mg

Thai Peanut, Carrot, and Shourimp Soup

Prep time: 10 minutes|Cook time: 10 minutes|Serves 4

- 1 tablespoon coconut oil
- 1 tablespoon Thai red curry paste
- ½ onion, sliced
- 3 garlic cloves, minutesced
- 2 cups chopped carrots
- ½ cup whole unsalted peanuts
- 4 cups low-sodium vegetable broth
- ½ cup unsweetened plain almond milk
- ½ pound shourimp, peeled and deveined
- minutesced fresh cilantro, for garnish

1. In a large pan, heat the oil over medium-high heat until shimmering.
2. Add the curry paste and Cook, stirring constantly, for 1 minutesute. Add the onion, garlic, carrots, and peanuts to the pan, and continue to Cook for 2 to 3 minutes until the onion begins to soften.
3. Add the broth and bring to a boil. Reduce the heat to low and simmer for 5 to 6 minutes until the carrots are tender.
4. Using an immersion blender or in a blender, purée the soup until smooth and return it to the pot. With the heat still on low, add the almond milk and stir to combine. Add the shourimp to the pot and Cook for 2 to 3 minutes until Cooked thourough.
5. Garnish with cilantro and serve.

PER SERVING

Calories 237| Cook Fat 14g| Protein 14g| Carbohydrates 17g| Sugars 6g| Fiber 5g| Sodium 619mg

Chicken Tortilla Soup

Prep time: 10 minutes|Cook time: 35 minutes|Serves 4

- 1 tablespoon extra-virgin olive oil
- 1 onion, thinly sliced
- 1 garlic clove, minutesced
- 1 jalapeño pepper, diced
- 2 boneless, skinless chicken breasts
- 4 cups low-sodium chicken broth
- 1 roma tomato, diced
- ½ teaspoon salt
- 2 (6-inch) corn tortillas, cut into thin strips
- Nonstick Cook spray
- Juice of 1 lime
- minutesced fresh cilantro, for garnish
- ¼ cup shouredded cheddar cheese, for garnish

1. In a medium pot, heat the oil over medium-high heat.
2. Add the onion and Cook for 3 to 5 minutes until it begins to soften.
3. Add the garlic and jalapeño, and Cook until fragrant, about 1 minutesute more.
4. Add the chicken, chicken broth, tomato, and salt to the pot and bring to a boil.
5. Reduce the heat to medium and simmer gently for 20 to 25 minutes until the chicken breasts are Cooked thourough.
6. Remove the chicken from the pot and set aside.
7. Preheat a broiler to high.
8. Spray the tortilla strips with nonstick Cook spray and toss to coat.
9. Spread in a single layer on a baking sheet and broil for 3 to 5 minutes, flipping once, until crisp.
10. When the chicken is cool enough to handle, shoured it with two forks and return to the pot.
11. Season the soup with the lime juice.
12. Serve hot, garnished with cilantro, cheese, and tortilla strips.

PER SERVING

Calories 191| Cook Fat 8g| Protein 19g| Carbohydrates 13g| Sugars 2g| Fiber 2g| Sodium 482mg

Meatball Vegetable Stew
Prep time: 15 minutes | Cook time: 25 minutes | Serves 2

- 1 lb. Sausage meat
- 2 cups chopped tomato
- 1 cup chopped vegetables
- 2 tablespoon Italian seasonings
- 1 tablespoon vegetable oil

1. Roll the sausage into meatballs.
2. Put the instant pot on sauté and fry the meatballs in the oil until brown.
3. Mix all the recipe ingredients in your instant pot.
4. Cook on stew for almost 25 minutes.
5. Release the pressure naturally.

PER SERVING

Calories 300| Cook Carbs 4g| Net Carbs 2g| Protein 40g| Fat 12g| Sugar 1g| Fiber 2g

Lentil Potato Stew
Prep time: 10 minutes | Cook time: 30 minutes | Serves 4

- 2 tablespoons avocado oil
- ½ cup diced onion
- 2 garlic cloves, crushed
- 1 to 1½ teaspoons sea salt
- 1 teaspoon black pepper
- 1 cup dry lentils
- 2 carrots, sliced
- 1 cup peeled and cubed potato
- 1 celery stalk, diced
- 2 oregano sprigs, chopped
- 2 tarragon sprigs, chopped
- 5 cups vegetable broth
- 1 (13.5-ounce) can skimmed coconut milk

1. In a great soup pot over average-high hotness, heat the avocado oil.
2. Add the garlic, onion, salt, and pepper, and sauté for 3 to 5 minutes, or until the onion is soft.
3. Add the lentils, carrots, potato, celery, oregano, tarragon, and 2½ cups of vegetable broth, and stir.
4. Get to a boil, decrease the heat to medium-low, and Cook, stirring frequently and adding additional vegetable broth a half cup at a time to make sure there is enough liquid for the lentils and potatoes to Cook, for almost 20 to 25 minutes, or until the potatoes and lentils are soft.
5. Take away from the heat, and stirring in the coconut milk.
6. Pour into 4 soup bowls and enjoy.

PER SERVING

Calories 85| Cook Carbs 20g| Net Carbs 2g| Protein 3g| Fat 2g| Sugar 1g| Fiber 2g

Tofu Soup
Prep time: 15 minutes | Cook time: 15 minutes | Serves 2

- 1 lb. minutesced tofu
- 0.5 lb. chopped vegetables
- 2 cups vegetable broth
- salt and Black pepper, to taste

1. Mix the tofu, flour, salt and pepper.
2. Form the meatballs from the mixture.
3. Place all the recipe ingredients in your instant pot.
4. Cook on stew for almost 15 minutes.
5. Release the pressure naturally.

PER SERVING

Calories 240| Cook Carbs 9g| Net Carbs 1.2g| Protein 35g| Fat 10g| Sugar 1g| Fiber 2g

Bacon Vegetable Stew
Prep time: 15 minutes | Cook time: 25 minutes | Serves 2

- 0.5 lb. soy bacon
- 1 lb. chopped vegetables
- 1 cup vegetable broth
- 1 tablespoon nutritional yeast

1. Mix all the recipe ingredients in your instant pot.
2. Cook on stew for almost 25 minutes.
3. Release the pressure naturally.

PER SERVING

Calories 200| Cook Carbs 12g| Fat 7| Net Carbs 0.5g| Protein 41| Sugar 1g| Fiber 2g

Bean Soup (Tuscan Style)
Prep time: 20 minutes | Cook time: 15 minutes|Cook time: 35 minutes | Serves 6

- 1 onion, chopped
- 2 cloves garlic, minutesced
- 3 cups of low fat, low sodium chicken broth
- 1 cup of canned whole tomatoes, chopped
- 2 teaspoons of chopped fresh thyme
- 1/2 cup of chopped spinach
- 1 cup of seashell whole-wheat pasta
- 1 tablespoon of olive oil

1. In a saucepan over medium-high heat, combine the onion, oil, and garlic and sauté for 5 minutes.
2. Add the red bell pepper and sauté for another 3 minutes.
3. Add the tomatoes, broth, and beans.
4. Bring to a boil, reduce heat to low, and simmer for 20 minutes.
5. Add spinach, thyme, and pasta.
6. Simmer for another 5 minutes. Serve!

PER SERVING

Calories 153| Protein 8g|Carbohydrates 29g| Fat 3.1g| Sodium 409.4mg

Cheesy Chicken Tortilla Soup

Prep time: 10 minutes | Cook time: 35 minutes | Serves 4

- 1 tablespoon extra-virgin olive oil
- 1 onion, thinly sliced
- 1 garlic clove, minutesced
- 1 jalapeño pepper, diced
- 2 boneless, skinless chicken breasts
- 4 cups low-sodium chicken broth
- 1 Roma tomato, diced
- ½ teaspoon salt
- 2 (6-inch) corn tortillas, cut into thin strips
- Nonstick Cook spray
- Juice of 1 lime
- minutesced fresh cilantro, for garnish
- ¼ cup shouredded Cheddar cheese, for garnish

1. In a medium pot, heat the oil over medium-high heat.
2. Add the onion and Cook for 3 to 5 minutes until it begins to soften.
3. Add the garlic and jalapeño, and Cook until fragrant, about 1 minutesute more.
4. Add the chicken, chicken broth, tomato, and salt to the pot and bring to a boil.
5. Reduce the heat to medium and simmer gently for 20 to 25 minutes until the chicken breasts are Cooked thourough.
6. Remove the chicken from the pot and set aside.
7. Preheat a broiler to high.
8. Spray the tortilla strips with nonstick Cook spray and toss to coat.
9. Spread in a single layer on a baking sheet and broil for 3 to 5 minutes, flipping once, until crisp.
10. When the chicken is cool enough to handle, shoured it with two forks and return to the pot.
11. Season the soup with the lime juice. Serve hot, garnished with cilantro, cheese, and tortilla strips.

PER SERVING

Calories 192 | Fat 8.1g | Protein 19.1g | Carbs 12.9g | Fiber 2.1g | Sugar 2.0g | Sodium 483mg

Taco Soup

Prep time: 5 minutes | Cook time: 20 minutes | Serves 4

- Avocado oil Cook spray
- 1 medium red bell pepper, chopped
- ½ cup chopped yellow onion
- 1 pound 93% lean ground beef
- 1 teaspoon ground cuminutes
- ½ teaspoon salt
- ½ teaspoon chili powder
- ½ teaspoon garlic powder
- 2 cups low-sodium beef broth
- 1 (15-ounce) can no-salt-added diced tomatoes
- 1½ cups frozen corn
- ⅓ cup half-and-half

1. Heat a large stockpot over medium-low heat.
2. When hot, coat the Cook surface with Cook spray.
3. Put the pepper and onion in the pan and Cook for 5 minutes.
4. Add the ground beef, cuminutes, salt, chili powder, and garlic powder. Cook for 5 to 7 minutes, stirring and breaking apart the beef as needed.
5. Add the broth, diced tomatoes with their juices, and corn. Increase the heat to medium-high and simmer for 10 minutes.
6. Remove from the heat and stir in the half-and-half.

PER SERVING

Calories 320| Cook Fat 12g| Protein 30g| Carbohydrates 23g| Sugars 7g| Fiber 4g| Sodium 456mg

Beef, Mushouroom, and Pearl Barley Soup

Prep time: 10 minutes | Cook time: 1 hour 20 minutes | Serves 6

- 1 pound (454 g) beef stew meat, cubed
- ¼ teaspoon salt
- ¼ teaspoon freshly ground black pepper
- 1 tablespoon extra-virgin olive oil
- 8 ounces (227 g) sliced mushourooms
- 1 onion, chopped
- 2 carrots, chopped
- 3 celery stalks, chopped
- 6 garlic cloves, minutesced
- ½ teaspoon dried thyme
- 4 cups low-sodium beef broth
- 1 cup water
- ½ cup pearl barley

1. Season the meat with the salt and pepper.
2. In an Instant Pot, heat the oil over high heat.
3. Add the meat and brown on all sides.
4. Remove the meat from the pot and set aside.
5. Add the mushourooms to the pot and Cook for 1 to 2 minutes, until they begin to soften.
6. Remove the mushourooms and set aside with the meat.
7. Add the onion, carrots, and celery to the pot. Sauté for 3 to 4 minutes until the vegetables begin to soften.
8. Add the garlic and continue to Cook until fragrant, about 30 seconds longer.
9. Return the meat and mushourooms to the pot, then add the thyme, beef broth, and water.
10. Set the pressure to high and Cook for 15 minutes. Let the pressure release naturally.
11. Open the Instant Pot and add the barley. Use the slow Cooker function on the Instant Pot, affix the lid (vent open), and continue to Cook for 1 hour until the barley is Cooked thourough and tender. Serve.

PER SERVING

Calories 250 | Fat 9.1g | Protein 21.1g | Carbs 18.9g | Fiber 4.1g | Sugar 3.0g | Sodium 515mg

Lamb and Vegetable Stew
Prep time: 10 minutes | Cook time: 3 to 6 hours | Serves 6

- 1 pound (454 g) boneless lamb stew meat
- 1 pound (454 g) turnips, peeled and chopped
- 1 fennel bulb, trimmed and thinly sliced
- 10 ounces (283 g) mushourooms, sliced
- 1 onion, diced
- 3 garlic cloves, minutesced
- 2 cups low-sodium chicken broth
- 2 tablespoons tomato paste
- ¼ cup dry red wine (optional)
- 1 teaspoon chopped fresh thyme
- ½ teaspoon salt
- ¼ teaspoon freshly ground black pepper
- Chopped fresh parsley, for garnish

1. In a slow Cooker, combine the lamb, turnips, fennel, mushourooms, onion, garlic, chicken broth, tomato paste, red wine (if using), thyme, salt, and pepper.
2. Cover and Cook on high for 3 hours or on low for 6 hours. When the meat is tender and falling apart, garnish with parsley and serve.
3. If you don't have a slow Cooker, in a large pot, heat 2 teaspoons of olive oil over medium heat, and sear the lamb on all sides. Remove from the pot and set aside. Add the turnips, fennel, mushourooms, onion, and garlic to the pot, and Cook for 3 to 4 minutes until the vegetables begin to soften. Add the chicken broth, tomato paste, red wine (if using), thyme, salt, pepper, and browned lamb. Bring to a boil, then reduce the heat to low. Simmer for 1½ to 2 hours until the meat is tender. Garnish with parsley and serve.

PER SERVING

Calories 305 | Fat 7.1g | Protein 32.1g | Carbs 26.9g | Fiber 4.1g | Sugar 7.0g | Sodium 312mg

Leek and Cauliflower Soup
Prep time: 10 minutes | Cook time: 20 minutes | Serves 2

- Avocado oil Cook spray
- 2½ cups chopped leeks (2 to 3 leeks)
- 2½ cups cauliflower florets
- 1 garlic clove, peeled
- ⅓ cup low-sodium vegetable broth
- ½ cup half-and-half
- ¼ teaspoon salt
- ¼ teaspoon freshly ground black pepper

1. Heat a large stockpot over medium-low heat.
2. When hot, coat the Cook surface with Cook spray.
3. Put the leeks and cauliflower into the pot.
4. Increase the heat to medium and cover the pan.
5. Cook for 10 minutes, stirring halfway thourough.
6. Add the garlic and Cook for 5 minutes.
7. Add the broth and deglaze the pan, stirring to scrape up the browned bits from the bottom.
8. Transfer the broth and vegetables to a food processor or blender and add the half-and-half, salt, and pepper. Blend well.

PER SERVING

Calories 174 | Fat 7.1g | Protein 6.1g | Carbs 23.9g | Fiber 5.1g | Sugar 8.0g | Sodium 490mg

French Onion Gruyere Soup
Prep time: 35 minutes | Cook time: 35 minutes | Serves 2

- 6 onions, chopped
- 2 cups vegetable broth
- 2 tablespoon oil
- 2 tablespoon gruyere

1. Place the oil in your instant pot and Cook the onions on sauté until soft and brown.
2. Mix all the recipe ingredients in your instant pot.
3. Cook on stew for 35 minutes.
4. Release the pressure naturally.

PER SERVING

Calories 110| Cook Carbs 8| Net Carbs 3g| Protein 3g| Fat 10| Sugar 1g| Fiber 2g

Chicken Zucchini Noodle Soup
Prep time: 15 minutes | Cook time: 35 minutes | Serves 2

- 1 lb. Cooked chicken, chopped
- 1 lb. zucchini, spiralized
- 1 cup chicken soup
- 1 cup diced vegetables

1. Mix all the recipe ingredients except the zucchini in your instant pot.
2. Cook on stew for 35 minutes.
3. Release the pressure naturally.
4. Stir in the zucchini and allow to heat thoroughly.

PER SERVING

Calories 250| Cook Carbs 5g| Sugar 0g| Fat 10g| Net Carbs 2g| Protein 40g| Sugar 1g| Fiber 2g

Chicken Coconut Soup

Prep time: 15 minutes | Cook time: 30 minutes|Cook time: 45 minutes | Serves 6

- 1-inch piece ginger, peeled and minutesced
- 1 medium zucchini, cut into quarters lengthwise and diced
- 0.75 pound of pumpkin, cubed into 1/2-inch pieces (1 cup)
- 1 red bell pepper, seeds removed and thinly sliced
- 1 pound of chicken breast, thinly sliced
- Salt & pepper, to taste
- 2 cups of chicken broth
- Juice of 1 lime
- Handful cilantro leaves (optional)
- 1 tablespoon of coconut oil (or vegetable oil)
- 1 small onion, thinly sliced into half-moons
- 2 garlic cloves, minutesced
- 1 small chili or jalapeño pepper, seeds removed and thinly sliced
- 14 ounces of lite coconut milk (1 can)

1. Season the sliced chicken breast generously with pepper and salt.
2. In a large (5 to 6 quart) soup pot, heat the coconut oil over high heat and add the chicken breast. Stir-fry over high heat until the chicken is no longer pink outside or for about 4 to 5 minutes.
3. Add the minutesced garlic, sliced onion, and chopped ginger. Continue to sauté for another 2-3 minutes.
4. Next, add the diced squash, diced zucchini and then stir.
5. Add the sliced chili or jalapeno, chicken broth, sliced bell pepper the coconut milk and lime juice. Give everything another good stir.
6. Bring to a boil, lower the heat, cover and simmer until the squash is fully Cooked.
7. Remove from heat and season with more pepper and salt, if desired. Garnish with cilantro leaves to serve.
8. Serve and enjoy!

PER SERVING

Calories 231|Fat 12.7g|Cholesterol 3.7mg|Carbohydrates 11.6g|Fiber 1.7g|Sugar 5g| Protein 17.1g

Cucumber, Tomato, and Avocado Salad

Prep time: 10 minutes|Cook time:30 miutes|Serves 4

- 1 cup cherry tomatoes, halved
- 1 large cucumber, chopped
- 1 small red onion, thinly sliced
- 1 avocado, diced
- 2 tablespoons chopped fresh dill
- 2 tablespoons extra-virgin olive oil
- Juice of 1 lemon
- ¼ teaspoon salt
- ¼ teaspoon freshly ground black pepper

1. In a large mixing bowl, combine the tomatoes, cucumber, onion, avocado, and dill.
2. In a small bowl, combine the oil, lemon juice, salt, and pepper, and mix well.
3. Drizzle the dressing over the vegetables and toss to combine. Serve.

PER SERVING

Calories 151| Cook Fat 12g| Protein 2g| Carbohydrates 11g| Sugars 4g| Fiber 4g| Sodium 128mg

Cabbage Slaw Salad

Prep time: 15 minutes|Cook time:30 minutes|Serves 6

- 2 cups finely chopped green cabbage
- 2 cups finely chopped red cabbage
- 2 cups grated carrots
- 3 scallions, both white and green parts, sliced
- 2 tablespoons extra-virgin olive oil
- 2 tablespoons rice vinegar
- 1 teaspoon honey
- 1 garlic clove, minutesced
- ¼ teaspoon salt

1. In a large bowl, toss together the green and red cabbage, carrots, and scallions.
2. In a small bowl, whisk together the oil, vinegar, honey, garlic, and salt.
3. Pour the dressing over the veggies and mix to thoroughly combine.
4. Serve immediately, or cover and chill for several hours before serving.

PER SERVING

Calories 80| Cook Fat 5g| Protein 1g| Carbohydrates 10g| Sugars 6g| Fiber 3g| Sodium 126mg

Chicken Noodle Soup

Prep time: 15 minutes | Cook time: 35 minutes | Cook time: 50 minutes | Serves 8

- 1 teaspoon of dried parsley
- 1 teaspoon of garlic powder
- 1/2 teaspoon of poultry seasoning
- 1/2 teaspoon of salt
- 1 cup of diced onion (approximately 1/2 large onion)
- 1/2 cup of finely diced celery
- 1/8 teaspoon of black pepper
- 4 ounces of dry angel hair pasta (break noodles in half)
- 2 (8 ounces each) boneless, skinless chicken breasts
- 6 cups of water
- 1 can (14 1/2 ounces) of fat-free, 1/3 less-sodium chicken broth
- 1/3 cup of finely diced carrot

1. Place the chicken, water, onion, celery, broth, and carrot in a one-gallon pot and bring to a boil.
2. Cook until the chicken is no longer pink (about 15 minutes).
3. Remove chicken and skim any fat from broth (or refrigerate broth for 2 to 3 hours and then skim fat).
4. Dice chicken into bite-size pieces.
5. Return chicken to the skimmed broth along with all remaining ingredients. Place over high heat and return to a boil.
6. Reduce heat to medium-high and boil.
7. Gently for about 3-5 minutes, until pasta is Cooked
8. Serve right away; the pasta will continue to absorb liquid if the soup is left simmering.

PER SERVING

Calories 151| Carbs 10 g|Protein 21 g|Fat 3 g| Sodium 276 mg|Fiber 1g

Golden Soup

Prep time: 10 minutes | Cook time: 10 minutes | Cook time: 20 minutes | Serves 6

- pinch dry, mixed herbs
- 1 heaped teaspoon of nutritional yeast
- spray oil (optional)
- 1 low-salt stock cube (optional)
- 500ml of boiling water
- 1 red onion
- 1 white onion
- 1 red pepper
- 2 yellow/orange peppers
- 2 large or 4 small courgettes
- 2 tomatoes

1. Preheat oven to 375 degrees f.
2. Cut all the vegetables into chunks, sprinkle with dried mixed herbs and nutritional yeast, spray oil to speed up the roasting process.
3. Place in the center of the oven for 25-30 minutes until the vegetables are bronzed and browned on the edges.
4. Separately stir the broth into the hot water, ready to add to the Blitzer.
5. Stir and whisk and pour into a skillet, and heat thourough. Check the seasoning, serve!

PER SERVING

Calories 63|Carbohydrates 9.5g|Fiber 3.7g| Protein 2.5g| Fat 0.8g|Sugars 7.8g

Spring Vegetable Soup

Prep time: 4 minutes | Cook time: 10 minutes | Cook time: 14 minutes | Serves 4

- 1 cup of baby carrots, halved lengthwise and cut into 1-inch lengths
- 1/4 teaspoon of salt
- 1 1/2 tablespoons of fresh lemon juice
- 1/4 cup of thinly sliced fresh basil leaves
- 1/4 teaspoon of freshly ground black pepper
- 1/4 pound of thin asparagus (about 10 spears), trimmed and cut into 1-inch lengths
- 1/4 cup of coarsely shouredded Parmesan cheese
- 2 teaspoons of olive oil
- 1/2 sweet onion, chopped
- 1 garlic clove, minutesced
- 4 cups of low-sodium vegetable broth
- 1 cup of fresh shelled green peas or frozen petite peas
- 1 tightly packed cup of baby spinach

1. Preheat oven to 425°F. Line a baking sheet with parchment paper.
2. Sprinkle the cheese on the baking sheet, making a Cook of 4 piles.
3. Spread each pile into a 3-inch (8cm) round. Bake until cheese is lightly browned on the edges.
4. Meanwhile, to make the soup, place a large saucepan over medium heat and add the oil.
5. Add the onion and Cook, often stirring until softened, about 5 minutes.
6. Add the garlic and Cook, stirring, until fragrant, 30 seconds.
7. Add the broth and bring to a boil. Add the salt, carrots, and pepper. Cover, reduce heat, and simmer until carrots are tender about 5 minutes.
8. Add the peas and asparagus, and Cook until crisp-tender, about 2 minutes.
9. Remove the saucepan from the heat and stir in the lemon juice and spinach. Pour the soup into 4 bowls.
10. Top each bowl with a parmesan crisp and sprinkle with 1 tablespoon basil. Serve immediately and enjoy!

PER SERVING

Calories 99|Fat 4g| Carbs 15g| Sugar 0mg| Protein 5g

Chapter 7
Chicken and Poultry

Chicken Loaf

Prep time: 25 minutes | Cook time: 25 minutes | Serves 4

- 4 ounces of chopped raw carrots
- 1 cup of chopped raw celery
- 1 tablespoon of dehydrated onions
- 1 small can of pimento, chopped
- 4 tablespoon of diet mayonnaise
- 1 1/2 cup of water
- 2 packets of or cubes chicken bouillon
- 3 envelopes unflavored gelatin
- 1 teaspoon of garlic salt
- 2 tablespoons of mustard
- 1 teaspoon of lemon pepper
- 1 teaspoon of salt
- 1/2 teaspoon of pepper
- 16 ounces of Cooked, chopped chicken

1. Mix all ingredients except bouillon, water, and gelatin.
2. Dissolve bouillon in 1 cup water.
3. Dissolve gelatin in the remaining 1/2 cup of water.
4. Add gelatin to boiling bouillon. Add to mixture.
5. Pour into the loaf pan. Refrigerate.
6. Un-mold, slice, and serve.

PER SERVING

Calories 37| Protein 5.6 g| Fat 0.5g| Saturated Fat 0.2 g| Carbohydrate 1.9g| Sugars 0.1g|Potassium 129mg

Peanut Chicken Satay

Prep time: 20 minutes, plus 2 hours to marinate|Cook time: 10 minutes|Serves 8

- FOR THE PEANUT SAUCE
- 1 cup natural peanut butter
- 2 tablespoons low-sodium tamari or gluten-free soy sauce
- 1 teaspoon red chili paste
- 1 tablespoon honey
- Juice of 2 limes
- ½ cup hot water
- FOR THE CHICKEN
- 2 pounds boneless, skinless chicken thighs, trimmed of fat and cut into 1-inch pieces
- ½ cup plain nonfat Greek yogurt
- 2 garlic cloves, minutesced
- 1 teaspoon minutesced fresh ginger
- ½ onion, coarsely chopped
- 1½ teaspoons ground coriander
- 2 teaspoons ground cuminutes
- ½ teaspoon salt
- 1 teaspoon extra-virgin olive oil
- Lettuce leaves, for serving

1. In a large mixing bowl, combine the chicken, yogurt, garlic, ginger, onion, coriander, cuminutes, and salt, and mix well.
2. Cover and marinate in the refrigerator for at least 2 hours.
3. Thouread the chicken pieces onto bamboo skewers.
4. In a grill pan or large skillet, heat the oil. Cook the skewers for 3 to 5 minutes on each side until the pieces are Cooked thourough.
5. Remove the chicken from the skewers and place a few pieces on each lettuce leaf. Drizzle with the peanut sauce and serve.

PER SERVING

Calories 386| Cook Fat 26g| Protein 30g| Carbohydrates 14g| Sugars 6g| Fiber 2g| Sodium 442mg

Onion Fried Chicken

Prep time: 15 minutes | Cook time: 30 minutes|Cook time: 45 minutes | Serves 12

- 1 broiler (2 1/2 to 3 pounds cut up)
- 1 teaspoon of salt
- 1/2 teaspoon of pepper
- 2 onions, peeled and sliced
- 1/2 cup of water

1. Skin chicken. Place chicken in a non-stick pan.
2. Sprinkle with salt and pepper, and place onion on top.
3. Cover, Cook on low heat for 30 minutes.
4. Tilt lid so liquid will evaporate.
5. Continue Cook for 20 minutes or until tender.
6. Place chicken on the platter.
7. Return onions, add water, Cook until thickened.

PER SERVING

Calories 310|Fat 14g| Saturated fat 3g| Protein 31g| Carbs 15.5g| Fiber 1g|Cholesterol 79mg

Chicken Tuscany

Prep time: 10 minutes| Cook time: 15 minutes| Serves 4

- 1½ lbs. chicken breasts, boneless, skinless and sliced thin
- 1 cup spinach, chopped
- 1 cup half-n-half
- What you'll need from store cupboard:
- ½ cup reduced fat parmesan cheese
- ½ cup low sodium chicken broth
- ½ cup sun dried tomatoes
- 2 tbsp. olive oil
- 1 tsp Italian seasoning
- 1 tsp garlic powder

1. Heat oil in a large skillet over med-high heat.
2. Add chicken and Cook 3-5 minutes per side, or until browned and Cooked thourough. Transfer to a plate.
3. Add half-n-half, broth, cheese and seasonings to the pan.
4. Whisk constantly until sauce starts to thicken.
5. Add spinach and tomatoes and Cook, stirring frequently, until spinach starts to wilt, about 2-3 minutes.
6. Add chicken back to the pan and Cook just long enough to heat thourough.

PER SERVING

Calories 462| Cook Carbs 6g |Net Carbs 5g| Protein 55g| Fat 23g |Sugar 0g |Fiber 1g

The Ultimate Type 2 Diabetes UK Cookbook for Beginners

Chicken Pappardelle

Prep time: 15 minutes | Cook time: 15 minutes | Serves 4

- ¾ lb. chicken breast, sliced lengthwise into 1/8-inch strips
- 1 small onion, sliced thin
- 8 cup spinach, chopped fine
- 4 cup low sodium chicken broth
- 1 cup fresh basil
- What you'll need from store cupboard:
- 2 quarts water
- ¼ cup reduced fat parmesan cheese, divided
- 6 cloves garlic, diced
- 1 tbsp. walnuts, chopped
- ¼ tsp cinnamon
- ¼ tsp paprika
- ¼ tsp red pepper flakes
- Salt
- Olive oil Cook spray

1. Bring 2 quarts water to a simmer in a medium pot.
2. Lightly spray a medium skillet with Cook spray and place over med-high heat.
3. Add the garlic and Cook until golden brown.
4. Add the cinnamon, paprika, red pepper flakes, basil leaves, and onion.
5. Cook until the onion has softened, about 2 minutes.
6. Add the spinach and Cook until it has wilted and softened, another 2 minutes.
7. Add the broth, bring to a simmer, cover, and Cook until tender, about 5 minutes.
8. Add a pinch of salt to the now-simmering water.
9. Turn off the heat and add the chicken and stir so that all the strips are separated.
10. Cook just until the strips have turned white; they will be half-Cooked. Using a slotted spoon, transfer the strips to a plate to cool.
11. Check the spinach mixture; Cook it until most of the broth has evaporated Stir in half the cheese and season with salt to taste.
12. Add the chicken, toss to coat, and continue to Cook until the chicken strips have Cooked thourough, about 90 seconds.
13. Spoon the mixture onto four plates, top with the remaining cheese and serve.

PER SERVING

Calories 174| Cook Carbs 7g| Net Carbs 5g| Protein 24g |Fat 5g| Sugar 2g |Fiber 2g

Stuffed Chicken Breasts

Prep time: 15 minutes | Cook time: 30 minutes | Serves 4

- 1 cup chopped roasted red pepper
- 2 ounces (57 g) low-fat goat cheese
- 4 Kalamata olives, pitted, finely chopped
- 1 tablespoon chopped fresh basil
- 4 (5-ounce / 142-g) boneless, skinless chicken breasts
- 1 tablespoon extra-virgin olive oil

1. Preheat the oven to 400 °F.
2. In a small bowl, combine the peppers, goat cheese, olives, and basil until blended.
3. Put the container in the refrigerator for 15 minutes to harden.
4. Cut the chicken breast horizontally and make a pocket in the middle. Distribute the filling evenly between the chicken breast pouches and secure with a wooden toothpicks.
5. Place a large saucepan over medium-high heat and pour in the olive oil. Cook chicken for a Cook of 10 minutes on both sides.
6. Transfer to the oven. Cook the chicken until Cooked thourough, about 20 minutes.
7. Let the chicken sit for 10 minutes, then remove the toothpicks before eating.

PER SERVING

Calories 246| Cook Carbs 3g| Net Carbs 2g| Protein 35g| Fat 9g| Sugar 2g| Fiber 1g

Chicken Salad

Prep time: 10 minutes|Cook time: 10 minutes | Serves 4

- 12 ounces of sliced chicken
- 1/2 cup of chopped celery
- 1/4 cup of shouredded carrots
- 1/4 cup of low-calorie salad dressing or mayonnaise
- 1 1/2 teaspoon of lime juice
- Salt & pepper to taste

1. Combine chicken celery and carrots.
2. Stir dressing, juice, salt, and pepper.
3. Pour over chicken mixture, tossing to coat well.

PER SERVING

Calories 300| Fat 18g| Saturated Fat 2.5g| Sodium 490mg| Carbohydrate 2g| Sugars 1g| Protein 28g

Chicken Stuffed with Mushourooms
Prep time: 15 minutes| Cook time: 3 hours| Serves 4

- 4 thin chicken breasts, boneless and skinless
- What you'll need from store cupboard:
- 1 small can mushourooms, drain and slice
- ½ cup + 2 tbsp. low sodium chicken broth
- ½ cup fine bread crumbs
- 1 tbsp. dry white wine
- 1 tbsp. cornstarch
- ½ tsp sage
- ½ tsp garlic powder
- ¼ tsp marjoram
- Salt & pepper to taste

1. Place chicken between 2 sheets of plastic wrap and pound to 1/8-inch thick, working from the center to the edges.
2. In a small bowl, combine mushourooms, bread crumbs, 2 tablespoons broth and seasonings.
3. Spoon one fourth stuffing mix onto short end of chicken breast. Fold long sides in and roll up. Secure with toothpick.
4. Place chicken in crock pot and add the ½ cup broth.
5. Cover and Cook on high 3 hours, or until chicken is Cooked thourough.
6. Transfer chicken to a plate and tent with foil to keep warm.
7. Place over medium heat. In a small bowl, whisk together the wine and cornstarch.
8. Add to the saucepan and Cook, stirring constantly, until sauce is bubbly and thick. Cook 2 minutes more. Spoon sauce over chicken and serve.

PER SERVING

Calories 181| Cook Carbs 13g| Net Carbs 12g| Protein 28g| Fat 2g |Sugar 1g |Fiber 1g

Chicken Stew
Prep time: 10 minutes | Cook time: 1 hour |Cook time: 1hour 10 minutes | Serves 4

- 4 chicken breasts, stewed
- 1 (6 ounces of) can of mushourooms
- 1/2 medium head cabbage, chopped
- 2 medium onions, chopped
- Salt, pepper, and garlic to taste
- 1 (12 ounces of) tomato juice

1. To stew the chicken, cover with water and pressure for 15 minutes.
2. Remove chicken from water, add cabbage, mushourooms, and onions.
3. Add pepper, salt, and garlic to taste.
4. Add tomato juice and shouredded chicken.
5. Simmer for about 1 hour. Serve.

PER SERVING

Calories 684| Fat 32g| Saturated Fat 8.8g| Sodium 942mg| Carbohydrate 33g| Sugars 5.5g| Protein 64g

Chicken Marsala
Prep time: 10 minutes| Cook time: 25 minutes| Serves 4

- 4 boneless chicken breasts
- ½ lb. mushourooms, sliced
- 1 tbsp. margarine
- What you'll need from store cupboard:
- 1 cup Marsala wine
- ¼ cup flour
- 1 tbsp. oil
- Pinch of white pepper
- Pinch of oregano
- Pinch of basil

1. On a shallow plate, combine flour and seasonings.
2. Dredge the chicken in the flour mixture to coat both sides.
3. In a large skillet, over medium heat, heat oil until hot.
4. Add chicken and Cook until brown on both sides, about 15 minutes. Transfer chicken to a plate.
5. Reduce heat to low and add mushourooms and ¼ cup of the wine.
6. Cook about 5 minutes. Scrape bottom of pan to loosen any flour.
7. Stir in reserved flour mixture and the remaining wine.
8. Simmer until mixture starts to thicken, stirring constantly.
9. Add the chicken back to the pan and Cook an additional 5 minutes. Serve.

PER SERVING

Calories 327 |Cook Carbs 9g |Net Carbs 8g| Protein 21g| Fat 14g |Sugar 1g |Fiber 1g

Turkey and Avocado Patties
Cook time:3-4minutes|Serves 4

- Ground turkey, (93% lean) - 8 ounces
- Avocado (chopped) - ½
- Egg - 1
- Garlic - 1 clove
- Salt - as per taste
- Pepper - as per taste
- Olive oil Cook spray

1. Start by taking a large mixing bowl.
2. Add in the ground turkey, chopped garlic, egg, pepper, and salt. Mix well.
3. Now add in the chopped avocado and gently fold it with the turkey mixture.
4. Divide the mixture into 2 equal halves and mold each half into a patty.
5. Take a nonstick pan and grease it with olive oil Cook spray.
6. Place the patties in the pan and Cook for about 3-4 minutes on each side over a medium flame. =

PER SERVING

Fat 15.4 g |Protein 26 g |Carbohydrates 4.2 g

Chicken Zucchini Patties with Salsa
Prep time: 10 minutes| Cook time: 10 minutes| Serves 8

- 2 cup chicken breast, Cooked, divided
- 1 zucchini, cut in ¾-inch pieces
- ¼ cup cilantro, diced
- What you'll need from store cupboard:
- 1/3 cup bread crumbs
- 1/3 cup lite mayonnaise
- 2 tsp olive oil
- ½ tsp salt
- ¼ tsp pepper
- Roasted Tomato Salsa, (chapter 16)

1. Place 1 ½ cups chicken and zucchini into a food processor.
2. Cover and process until coarsely chopped.
3. Add bread crumbs, mayonnaise, pepper, cilantro, remaining chicken, and salt. Cover and pulse until chunky.
4. Heat oil in a large skillet over med-high heat.
5. Shape chicken mixture into 8 patties and Cook 4 minutes per side, or until golden brown.
6. Serve topped with salsa.

PER SERVING

Calories 146| Cook Carbs 10g| Net Carbs 8g |Protein 12g| Fat 7g |Sugar 5g |Fiber 2g

Easy Chicken Cacciatore
Prep time: 10 minutes|Cook time: 45 minutes|Serves 6

- 3 teaspoons extra-virgin olive oil, divided
- 6 chicken legs
- 8 ounces brown mushourooms
- 1 large onion, sliced
- 1 red bell pepper, seeded and cut into strips
- 3 garlic cloves, minutesced
- ½ cup dry red wine
- 1 (28-ounce) can whole tomatoes, drained
- 1 thyme sprig
- 1 rosemary sprig
- ½ teaspoon salt
- ¼ teaspoon freshly ground black pepper
- ¼ cup water

1. Preheat the oven to 350°F.
2. In a Dutch oven (or any oven-safe covered pot), heat 2 teaspoons of oil over medium-high heat.
3. Sear the chicken on all sides until browned. Remove and set aside.
4. Heat the remaining 1 teaspoon of oil in the Dutch oven and sauté the mushourooms for 3 to 5 minutes until they brown and begin to release their water.
5. Add the onion, bell pepper, and garlic, and mix together with the mushourooms.
6. Cook an additional 3 to 5 minutes until the onion begins to soften.
7. Add the red wine and deglaze the pot. Bring to a simmer. Add the tomatoes, breaking them into pieces with a spoon. Add the thyme, rosemary, salt, and pepper to the pot and mix well.
8. Add the water, then nestle the Cooked chicken, along with any juices that have accumulated, in the vegetables.
9. Transfer the pot to the oven.
10. Cook for 30 minutes until the chicken is Cooked thourough and its juices run clear.
11. Remove the thyme and rosemary sprigs and serve.

PER SERVING

Calories 257| Cook Fat 11g| Protein 28g| Carbohydrates 11g| Sugars 6g| Fiber 2g| Sodium 398mg

Chicken Salad with Fruits
Prep time: 10 minutes|Cook time: 10 minutes | Serves 4

- 3 ounces of blended cottage cheese
- 2 tablespoons of skim milk
- 1 tablespoon of cider vinegar
- 2 teaspoon of grated onion
- 1 teaspoon of salt
- 1 med. green pear, cubed
- 1 med. apple, cubed
- 1 cup of chopped celery
- Lettuce leaves

1. Mix celery, apple, pear, chicken, and salt until smooth.
2. Add onion, vinegar, milk, and cheese and toss.
3. Serve on lettuce leaves.

PER SERVING

Calories 231| Fat 8.9g| Saturated fat 1.5g| Protein 22.5g| Carbohydrates 15.5g| Fiber 1.7g| Calcium 30mg

Chicken & Spinach Pasta Skillet

Prep time: 10 minutes | Cook time: 15 minutes | Serves 4

- 1 lb. chicken, boneless, skinless, cut into 1-inch pieces
- 10 cup fresh spinach, chopped
- 1 lemon, juiced and zested
- What you'll need from store cupboard:
- ½ recipe homemade pasta, (chapter 14) Cook and drain
- ½ cup dry white wine
- 4 cloves garlic, diced fine
- 4 tbsp. reduced fat parmesan cheese, divided
- 2 tbsp. extra-virgin olive oil
- ½ tsp salt
- ¼ tsp ground pepper

1. Heat oil in a large, deep skillet over med-high heat. Add chicken, salt and pepper.
2. Cook, stirring occasionally, until just Cooked thourough, 5-7 minutes.
3. Add garlic and Cook, stirring, until fragrant, about 1 minutesute.
4. Stir in wine, lemon juice and zest; bring to a simmer.
5. Remove from heat. Stir in spinach and pasta.
6. Cover and let stand until the spinach is just wilted.
7. Divide among 4 plates and top each serving with 1 tablespoon Parmesan.

PER SERVING

Calories 415 |Cook Carbs 12g |Net Carbs 9g| Protein 40g| Fat 19g| Sugar 4g |Fiber 3g

Roasted Chicken with Root Vegetables

Prep time: 20 minutes | Cook time: 41 minutes | Serves 6

- 1 teaspoon minutesced fresh rosemary
- 1 teaspoon minutesced fresh thyme
- 1 teaspoon salt
- 1 teaspoon ground black pepper
- 2 tablespoons olive oil, divided
- 6 (6-ounce / 170-g) boneless, skinless chicken breast halves
- 2 medium fennel bulbs, chopped
- 4 medium peeled carrots, chopped
- 3 peeled medium radishes, chopped
- 3 tablespoons honey
- ½ cup white wine
- 2 cups chicken stock
- 3 bay leaves

1. Preheat the oven to 375°F (190°C).
2. Mix the rosemary, thyme, salt, and black pepper in a small bowl.
3. Heat 1 tablespoon of olive oil in a nonstick skillet over medium-high heat until shimmering.
4. On a clean work surface, rub the chicken breasts with half of the seasoning mixture.
5. Place the chicken in the skillet and Cook for 6 minutes or until lightly browned on both sides.
6. Remove the chicken from the skillet and set aside.
7. Mix the fennel bulbs, carrots, and radishes in a microwave-safe bowl, then sprinkle with remaining seasoning mixture and drizzle with honey, white wine, and remaining olive oil. Toss to combine well.
8. Cover the bowl and microwave the root vegetables for 10 minutes or until soft.
9. Arrange the root vegetables and chicken in a baking sheet, then pour in the chicken stock and honey mixture remains in the bowl. Top them with bay leaves.
10. Place the sheet in the preheated oven and roast for 25 minutes or until the internal temperature of the chicken reaches at least 165°F (74°C).
11. Remove the sheet from the oven and transfer the chicken and vegetables on a large plate.
12. Discard the bay leaves, then allow to cool for a few minutes before serving.

PER SERVING

Calories 364 | Fat 10.2g | Protein 41.8g | Carbs 22.2g | Fiber 3.8g | Sugar 15.1g | Sodium 650mg

Coconut Crusted Chicken Tenders

Prep time: 10 minutes | Cook time: 20 minutes | Serves 6

- 4 chicken breasts each cut lengthwise into 3 strips
- ½ teaspoon salt
- ¼ teaspoon black pepper
- ½ cup coconut flour
- 2 eggs, beaten
- 2 tablespoons unsweetened plain almond milk
- 1 cup unsweetened coconut flakes

1. At 400 degrees F, preheat your oven.
2. Layer a suitable baking sheet with parchment paper.
3. Season the sliced chicken pieces with black pepper and salt.
4. Place the coconut flour in a suitable bowl. In another bowl, mix the eggs with the almond milk.
5. Spread the coconut flakes on a plate. One by one, roll the chicken pieces in the flour, then dip the floured chicken in the egg mixture and shake off any excess.
6. Roll in the coconut flakes and transfer to the Prepared baking sheet.
7. Bake for almost 15 to 20 minutes, flipping once halfway thourough until Cooked thourough and browned.

PER SERVING

Calories 216| Fats 13g| Net Carbs 1g| Proteins 20g| Cook Carbs 9g |Fibers 6g| Sugars 2g

Lettuce Salad with Turkey

Prep time: 10 minutes | Cook time: 0 minutes | Serves 4

- 1 bibb or butterhead lettuce head, quartered
- 2 cups shouredded Cooked turkey breast
- 1 cup halved grape or cherry tomatoes
- 2 hard-Cooked eggs, chopped
- 4 slices low-sodium and less-fat bacon, crisp-Cooked, and crumbled
- ¼ cup chopped red onion
- Black pepper, to taste

1. Arrange 1 lettuce quarter on each plate.
2. Drizzle half of the dressing over wedges.
3. Top with turkey, eggs, and tomatoes.
4. Drizzle with the remaining dressing.
5. Sprinkle with onion, bacon and pepper. Serve.

PER SERVING

Calories 228| Cook Carb 8g| Net Carbs 1.2g| Fat 9g| Protein 29g| Fibers 3g| Sugars: 6g

Spatchcock with Lime Aioli

Prep time: 15 minutes | Cook time: 45 minutes | Serves 6

- 4 pounds (1.8 kg) chicken, spatchcocked
- 3 tablespoons blackened seasoning
- 2 tablespoons olive oil
- Lime Aioli:
- ½ cup lite mayonnaise
- Juice and zest of 1 lime
- ¼ teaspoon kosher salt
- ¼ teaspoon ground black pepper

1. Heat the grill to a medium-high heat in advance.
2. Rub the chicken with blackened seasoning and olive oil on a clean work surface.
3. Cook the chicken for 45 minutes on a hot grill, skin side up, or until the internal temperature reaches 165°F (74°C).
4. Meanwhile, in a small mixing bowl, add all of the aioli Ingredients and swirl well to combine.
5. Transfer the chicken to a large platter and baste with the lime aioli after it's finished grilling.
6. Allow to cool before serving.

PER SERVING

Calories 436| Cook Carbs 6.8g| Net Carbs 4.6g| Protein 61.1g| Fat 8.0g| Sugar 1.5g| Fiber 0.7 g

Carrots and Kale with Chicken

Prep time: 15 minutes| Cook time: 27 minutes | Serves 2

- ½ cup couscous
- 1 cup water, divided
- ⅓ cup basil pesto
- 3 teaspoons olive oil, divided
- 3 (2-ounce / 57-g) whole carrots, rinsed, thinly sliced
- Salt and ground black pepper, to taste
- 1 (about 6-ounce / 170-g) bunch kale, rinsed, stems removed, chopped
- 2 cloves garlic, minutesced
- 2 tablespoons dried currants
- 1 tablespoon red wine vinegar
- 2 (6-ounce / 170-g) boneless, skinless chicken breasts, rinsed
- 1 tablespoon Italian seasoning

1. In a pot, combine the couscous and ¾ cup of water.
2. On high heat, bring to a boil. Reduce the heat to a low setting.
3. Cook for 7 minutes, or until the liquid has almost completely evaporated.
4. Mix in the basil pesto and fluff with a fork. In a nonstick skillet, heat 1 teaspoon olive oil over medium-high heat until it shimmers.
5. Season with salt and pepper after adding the carrots Sauté the vegetables for 3 minutes, or until they are tender. Sauté the kale and garlic for 2 minutes, or until the kale has wilted somewhat.
6. Add the currents and the remaining water to the pan and Cook for 3 minutes, or until most of the liquid has evaporated.
7. Remove the pan from the heat and add the red wine vinegar, stirring constantly.
8. Place them in a large mixing bowl and cover with plastic wrap to keep warm. Rub the chicken with Italian seasoning, salt, and pepper on a clean work surface.
9. Clean the skillet and heat 2 teaspoons olive oil until it shimmers over medium-high heat.
10. Sear the chicken for 12 minutes, or until it is thoroughly browned.
11. Rotate the chicken midway thourough the Cook time.
12. Place the chicken on a big platter with the vegetables and couscous on top.
13. To serve, cut into slices.

PER SERVING

Calories 461| Cook Carbs 9g| Net Carbs 0g| Protein 57.0g| Fat 5.0g| Sugar 5g| Fiber 6.5 g

Ritzy Jerked Chicken Breasts

Prep time: 4 hours 10 minutes | Cook time: 15 minutes | Serves 4

- 2 habanero chile peppers, halved lengthwise, seeded
- ½ sweet onion, cut into chunks
- 1 tablespoon minutesced garlic
- 1 tablespoon ground allspice
- 2 teaspoons chopped fresh thyme
- ¼ cup freshly squeezed lime juice
- ½ teaspoon ground nutmeg
- ¼ teaspoon ground cinnamon
- 1 teaspoon freshly ground black pepper
- 2 tablespoons extra-virgin olive oil
- 4 (5-ounce / 142-g) boneless, skinless chicken breasts
- 2 cups fresh arugula
- 1 cup halved cherry tomatoes

1. Combine the habaneros, onion, garlic, allspice, thyme, lime juice, nutmeg, cinnamon, black pepper, and olive oil in a blender. Pulse to blender well.
2. Transfer the mixture into a large bowl or two medium bowls, then dunk the chicken in the bowl and press to coat well.
3. Put the bowl in the refrigerator and marinate for at least 4 hours.
4. Preheat the oven to 400°F (205°C).
5. Remove the bowl from the refrigerator, then discard the marinade.
6. Arrange the chicken on a baking sheet, then roast in the preheated oven for 15 minutes or until golden brown and lightly charred. Flip the chicken halfway thourough the Cook time.
7. Remove the baking sheet from the oven and let sit for 5 minutes. Transfer the chicken on a large plate and serve with arugula and cherry tomatoes.

PER SERVING

Calories 226 | Fat 9.0g | Pprotein 33.0g | Carbs 3.0g | Fiber 0g | Sugar 1.0g | Sodium 92mg

Roasted Vegetable and Chicken Tortillas

Prep time: 10 minutes | Cook time: 20 minutes | Serves 4

- 1 red bell pepper, seeded and cut into 1-inch-wide strips
- ½ small eggplant, cut into ¼-inch-thick slices
- ½ small red onion, sliced
- 1 medium zucchini, cut lengthwise into strips
- 1 tablespoon extra-virgin olive oil
- Salt and freshly ground black pepper, to taste
- 4 whole-wheat tortilla wraps
- 2 (8-ounce / 227-g) Cooked chicken breasts, sliced

1. Preheat the oven to 400°F (205°C). Line a baking sheet with aluminutesum foil.
2. Combine the bell pepper, eggplant, red onion, zucchini, and olive oil in a large bowl. Toss to coat well.
3. Pour the vegetables into the baking sheet, then sprinkle with salt and pepper.
4. Roast in the preheated oven for 20 minutes or until tender and charred.
5. Unfold the tortillas on a clean work surface, then divide the vegetables and chicken slices on the tortillas.
6. Wrap and serve immediately.

PER SERVING

Calories 483 | Fat 25.0g | Protein 20.0g | Carbs 45.0g | Fiber 3.0g | Sugar 4.0g | Sodium 730mg

The Ultimate Type 2 Diabetes UK Cookbook for Beginners

Chapter 8
Beef, Lamb and Pork

Bunless Sloppy Joes

Prep time: 15 minutes | Cook time: 40 minutes | Serves 6

- 6 small sweet potatoes
- 1 pound lean ground beef
- 1 onion, finely chopped
- 1 carrot, finely chopped
- ¼ cup finely chopped mushourooms
- ¼ cup finely chopped red bell pepper
- 3 garlic cloves, minutesced
- 2 teaspoons Worcestershire sauce
- 1 tablespoon white wine vinegar
- 1 (15-ounce) can low-sodium tomato sauce
- 2 tablespoons tomato paste

1. Preheat the oven to 400°F.
2. Place the sweet potatoes in a single layer in a baking dish. Bake for 25 to 40 minutes, depending on the size, until they are soft and Cooked thourough.
3. While the sweet potatoes are baking, in a large skillet, Cook the beef over medium heat until it's browned, breaking it apart into small pieces as you stir.
4. Add the onion, carrot, mushourooms, bell pepper, and garlic, and sauté briefly for 1 minutesute.
5. Stir in the Worcestershire sauce, vinegar, tomato sauce, and tomato paste. Bring to a simmer, reduce the heat, and Cook for 5 minutes for the flavors to meld.
6. Scoop ½ cup of the meat mixture on top of each baked potato and serve.

PER SERVING

Calories 372| Cook Fat 19g| Protein 16g| Carbohydrates 34g| Sugars 13g| Fiber 6g| Sodium 161mg

Easy Beef Curry

Prep time: 15 minutes | Cook time: 10 minutes | Serves 6

- 1 tablespoon extra-virgin olive oil
- 1 small onion, thinly sliced
- 2 teaspoons minutesced fresh ginger
- 3 garlic cloves, minutesced
- 2 teaspoons ground coriander
- 1 teaspoon ground cuminutes
- 1 jalapeño or serrano pepper, slit lengthwise but not all the way thourough
- ¼ teaspoon ground turmeric
- ¼ teaspoon salt
- 1 pound grass-fed sirloin tip steak, top round steak, or top sirloin steak, cut into bite-size pieces
- 2 tablespoons chopped fresh cilantro

1. In a large skillet, heat the oil over medium high.
2. Add the onion, and Cook for 3 to 5 minutes until browned and softened. Add the ginger and garlic, stirring continuously until fragrant, about 30 seconds.
3. In a small bowl, mix the coriander, cuminutes, jalapeño, turmeric, and salt. Add the spice mixture to the skillet and stir continuously for 1 minutesute.
4. Deglaze the skillet with about ¼ cup of water.
5. Add the beef and stir continuously for about 5 minutes until well-browned yet still medium rare.
6. Remove the jalapeño. Serve topped with the cilantro.

PER SERVING

Calories 140| Cook Fat 7g| Protein 18g| Carbohydrates 3g| Sugars 1g| Fiber 1g| Sodium 141mg

Asian-Style Grilled Beef Salad

Prep time: 15 minutes | Cook time: 15 minutes | Serves 4

- FOR THE DRESSING
- ¼ cup freshly squeezed lime juice
- 1 tablespoon low-sodium tamari or gluten-free soy sauce
- 1 tablespoon extra-virgin olive oil
- 1 garlic clove, minutesced
- 1 teaspoon honey
- ¼ teaspoon red pepper flakes
- FOR THE SALAD
- 1 pound grass-fed flank steak
- ¼ teaspoon salt
- Pinch freshly ground black pepper
- 6 cups chopped leaf lettuce
- 1 cucumber, halved lengthwise and thinly cut into half moons
- ½ small red onion, sliced
- 1 carrot, cut into ribbons
- ¼ cup chopped fresh cilantro

1. Season the beef on both sides with the salt and pepper.
2. Heat a skillet over high heat until hot. Cook the beef for 3 to 6 minutes per side, depending on preferred doneness. Set aside, tented with aluminutesum foil, for 10 minutes.
3. In a large bowl, toss the lettuce, cucumber, onion, carrot, and cilantro.
4. Slice the beef thinly against the grain and transfer to the salad bowl.
5. Drizzle with the dressing and toss. Serve.

PER SERVING

Calories 231| Cook Fat 10g| Protein 26g| Carbohydrates 10g| Sugars 4g| Fiber 2g| Sodium 349mg

Barbecue Pork Loin

Prep time: 10 minutes, plus 20 minutes marinating time | Cook time: 35 minutes | Serves 4

- 1½ pounds boneless pork sirloin roast
- 1 cup white vinegar
- 3 small garlic cloves, pressed
- 1 tablespoon Creole Seasoning
- ½ teaspoon smoked paprika
- ½ teaspoon cayenne pepper
- ½ cup Chicken Broth or store-bought low-sodium chicken broth, plus more as needed
- ½ cup Barbecue Sauce , plus more for serving

1. Preheat the oven to 400°F.
2. In a medium bowl, combine the pork, vinegar, and garlic. Set aside to marinate for 10 minutes.
3. Remove the pork from the marinade, shaking off any remaining vinegar, and transfer to a rimmed baking sheet.
4. Massage the pork all over with the Creole seasoning, paprika, and cayenne. Cover and set aside for 20 minutes.
5. In a Dutch oven, bring the broth to a simmer over high heat.
6. Add the pork and Cook for 2 to 3 minutes per side, or until lightly browned. If the broth runs low, to keep the pork moist, add ¼ cup when turning.
7. Cover the pot, transfer to the oven, and Cook for 30 minutes, or until the pork is opaque.
8. Cover with the barbecue sauce, return to the oven, and Cook for 5 to 7 minutes, or until a nice crust forms on the exterior.
9. Transfer the pork to a cutting board. Let rest for 5 to 10 minutes.
10. Slice the pork, and serve with extra barbecue sauce.

PER SERVING

Calories 204|Cook Fat 7g|Cholesterol 75mg|Sodium 134mg| Cook Carbohydrates 9g| Sugar 6g| Fiber 0g| Protein 23g

Corned Beef and Cabbage Soup with Barley

Prep time: 15 minutes|Cook time:20 minutes|Serves 4

- 2 tablespoons avocado oil
- 1 small onion, chopped
- 3 celery stalks, chopped
- 3 medium carrots, chopped
- ¼ teaspoon allspice
- 4 cups Chicken Bone Broth, Vegetable Broth, low-sodium store-bought beef broth, or water
- 4 cups sliced green cabbage (about ⅓ medium head)
- ¾ cup pearled barley
- 4 ounces Cooked corned beef, cut into thin strips or chunks
- Freshly ground black pepper

1. Set the electric pressure Cooker to the Sauté setting. When the pot is hot, pour in the avocado oil.
2. Sauté the onion, celery, and carrots for 3 to 5 minutes or until the vegetables begin to soften. Stir in the allspice. Hit Cancel.
3. Stir in the broth, cabbage, and barley.
4. Close and lock the lid of the pressure Cooker. Set the valve to sealing.
5. Cook on high pressure for 20 minutes.
6. When the Cook is complete, allow the pressure to release naturally for 10 minutes, then quick release any remaining pressure. Hit Cancel.
7. Once the pin drops, unlock and remove the lid.
8. Stir in the corned beef, season with pepper, and replace the lid. Let the soup sit for about 5 minutes to let the corned beef warm up.
9. Spoon into serving bowls and serve.

PER SERVING

Calories 321| Cook Fat 13g| Protein 11g| Carbohydrates 42g| Sugars 7g| Fiber 11g| Sodium 412mg

Korean-Inspired Beef

Prep time: 10 minutes | Cook time: 10 minutes | Serves 6

- ¼ cup low-sodium beef broth or Vegetable Broth
- ¼ cup low-sodium gluten-free tamari or soy sauce
- 2 tablespoons rice wine vinegar
- 2 teaspoons Sriracha sauce (optional)
- 2 tablespoons brown sugar
- 1 tablespoon sesame oil
- 3 tablespoons minutesced garlic
- 1 tablespoon peeled and minutesced fresh ginger
- ½ teaspoon onion powder
- 1 teaspoon freshly ground black pepper
- 2 pounds top round beef, cut into thin, 3-inch-long strips
- 2 tablespoons cornstarch
- 1 teaspoon sesame seeds
- 2 scallions, green parts only, thinly sliced

1. In a 2-cup measuring cup or medium bowl, whisk together the broth, tamari, vinegar, Sriracha (if using), brown sugar, sesame oil, garlic, ginger, onion powder, and pepper.
2. In the electric pressure Cooker, combine the beef and broth mixture; stir.
3. Close and lock the lid of the pressure Cooker. Set the valve to sealing.
4. Cook on high pressure for 10 minutes.
5. When the Cook is complete, hit Cancel and quick release the pressure.
6. Once the pin drops, unlock and remove the lid.
7. Using a slotted spoon, transfer the beef to a serving bowl. Hit Sauté/More.
8. In a small bowl, combine the cornstarch and 3 tablespoons of cold water to make a slurry. Whisk the cornstarch mixture into the liquid in the pot and Cook, stirring frequently, for about 2 minutes or until the sauce has thickened. Hit Cancel.
9. Pour the sauce over the beef and garnish with the sesame seeds and scallions.

PER SERVING

Calories 328| Cook Fat 15g| Protein 35g| Carbohydrates 13g| Sugars 4g| Fiber 2g| Sodium 490mg

Orange-Marinated Pork Tenderloin

Prep time: 10 minutes, plus 2 hours to marinate | Cook time: 30 minutes | Serves 4

- ¼ cup freshly squeezed orange juice
- 2 teaspoons orange zest
- 2 teaspoons minutesced garlic
- 1 teaspoon low-sodium soy sauce
- 1 teaspoon grated fresh ginger
- 1 teaspoon honey
- 1½ pounds pork tenderloin roast, trimmed of fat
- 1 tablespoon extra-virgin olive oil

1. In a small bowl, whisk together the orange juice, zest, garlic, soy sauce, ginger, and honey.
2. Pour the marinade into a resealable plastic bag and add the pork tenderloin.
3. Remove as much air as possible and seal the bag. Marinate the pork in the refrigerator, turning the bag a few times, for 2 hours.
4. Preheat the oven to 400°F.
5. Remove the tenderloin from the marinade and discard the marinade.
6. Place a large ovenproof skillet over medium-high heat and add the oil.
7. Sear the pork tenderloin on all sides, about 5 minutes in Cook.
8. Transfer the skillet to the oven and roast the pork until just Cooked thourough, about 25 minutes.
9. Let the meat stand for 10 minutes before serving.

PER SERVING

Calories 228| Cook Fat 9g| Cholesterol 82mg| Sodium 486mg| Cook Carbohydrates 4g| Sugar 3g| Fiber 0g| Protein 34g

Mushouroom Sauced Pork Chops

Prep time: 20 minutes | Cook time: 0 minutes | Cook time: 8 hours 20 minutes | Serves 6

- 1 (10.75 ounces) can of reduced-fat, reduced-sodium condensed cream of mushouroom soup
- 2 teaspoons of snipped fresh thyme or 3/4 teaspoon dried thyme, crushed
- 1/4 teaspoon of garlic powder
- 4 pork loin chops, cut 3/4 inch thick (about 2 pounds)
- 1 tablespoon of Cook oil
- 1 small onion, thinly sliced
- 2 tablespoons of quick-Cook tapioca
- 1-1/2 cups of sliced fresh mushourooms
- 6 Fresh thyme sprigs
- 1/2 cup of apple juice or apple cider
- 1-1/2 teaspoons of Worcestershire sauce

1. Trim fat from chops. In a large skillet, heat oil over medium heat.
2. Add chops; Cook until browned, turning to brown evenly.
3. Drain off fat. Place onion in a 3-1/2- or 4-quart slow Cooker.
4. Add chops. Using a mortar and pestle, crush tapioca.
5. Combine mushouroom soup, apple juice, Worcestershire sauce, tapioca, snipped or dried thyme, and garlic powder in a medium bowl.
6. Stir in mushourooms. Pour over chops in the slow Cooker.
7. Cover & Cook on a low-heat setting for about 8 to 9 hours or on a high-heat setting for 4 to 4-1/2 hours.
8. If desired, garnish with thyme sprigs. Serve

PER SERVING

Calories 220| Pprotein 26.5g| Carbohydrates 11.5g| Dietary fiber 0.9g| Sugars 3.8g| Fat 6.7g| Saturated fat 1.7g

Raspberry Lemon Glazed Pork Chops

Prep time: 25 minutes | Cook time: 0 minutes | Cook time: 25 minutes | Serves 4

- 1 teaspoon of finely shouredded lemon peel
- 1/2 teaspoon of coarsely ground black pepper
- 1/4 teaspoon of salt
- 1/4 teaspoon of allspice
- 4 bone-in pork chops, cut about 1/2-inch thick about 1 1/4 pounds)
- 1/4 to 1/3 cup of seedless raspberry fruit spread
- 3 tablespoons of hickory smoke-flavored barbecue sauce
- Nonstick Cook spray

1. Trim fat from pork chops. Set it aside.
2. Combine the barbecue sauce, fruit spread, and lemon peel; set it aside.
3. In a small bowl, combine black pepper, salt, and allspice.
4. Sprinkle on both sides of pork chops.
5. Coat a nonstick skillet with Cook spray and place over medium-high heat until hot.
6. Cook the pork for about 3 to 4 minutes on each side or until just beginning to brown. Remove the pork & set it aside on a separate plate.
7. Add the fruit spread mixture to the same skillet.
8. Cook and stir until heated thourough.
9. Add the pork chops and Cook 1 to 2 minutes or until pork chops are glazed, turning occasionally.
10. Place on serving platter and spoon any remaining glaze in a pan overall.

PER SERVING

Calories 153| Protein 20.6g| Carbohydrates 11.7g| Dietary fiber 0.3g| Sugars 11.8g| Fat 3.5g| Saturated fat 1.1g| Cholesterol 65.3mg

Homestyle Herb Meatballs

Prep time: 10 minutes | Cook time: 15 minutes | Serves 4

- ½ pound lean ground pork
- ½ pound lean ground beef
- 1 sweet onion, finely chopped
- ¼ cup bread crumbs
- 2 tablespoons chopped fresh basil
- 2 teaspoons minutesced garlic
- 1 egg
- Pinch sea salt
- Pinch freshly ground black pepper

1. Preheat the oven to 350°F.
2. Line a baking tray with parchment paper and set it aside.
3. In a large bowl, mix together the pork, beef, onion, bread crumbs, basil, garlic, egg, salt, and pepper until very well mixed.
4. Roll the meat mixture into 2-inch meatballs.
5. Transfer the meatballs to the baking sheet and bake until they are browned and Cooked thourough, about 15 minutes.
6. Serve the meatballs with your favorite marinara sauce and some steamed green beans.

PER SERVING

Calories 332| Cook Fat 19g| Cholesterol 130mg| Sodium 188mg| Cook Carbohydrates 13g| Sugar 3g| Fiber 1g| Protein 24g

Pulled Pork Loin

Prep time: 30 minutes | Cook time: 35 minutes | Serves 4

- 2 pounds boneless pork sirloin roast
- 1 tablespoon ground mustard seeds
- ½ cup Chicken Broth (here) or store-bought low-sodium chicken broth
- 1 medium zucchini, grated
- 1 medium carrot, grated
- 1 medium onion, chopped
- 2 medium tomatoes, chopped
- ½ cup tomato paste
- ½ cup apple cider vinegar
- 2 tablespoons Pepper Sauce
- 1 tablespoon Worcestershire sauce
- 2 garlic cloves, minutesced
- 1 teaspoon Not Old Bay Seasoning

1. Massage the pork all over with the mustard seeds, and set aside for 20 minutes.
2. Select the Sauté setting on an electric pressure Cooker, and combine the chicken broth, zucchini, carrot, onion, tomatoes, tomato paste, vinegar, pepper sauce, Worcestershire sauce, garlic, and seasoning.
3. Cook, stirring often, for 5 minutes, or until the vegetables are softened.
4. Add the pork, close and lock the lid, and set the pressure valve to sealing.
5. Change to the Manual/Pressure Cook setting, and Cook for 30 minutes.
6. Once Cook is complete, quick-release the pressure. Carefully remove the lid.
7. Transfer the pork to a clean, flat surface, and shoured the meat using two forks.
8. Return the pork to the pressure Cooker and mix into the juices.
9. Serve with Savory Skillet Corn Bread and Spicy Mustard Greens.

PER SERVING

Calories 282| Cook Fat 19g| Cholesterol 70mg| Sodium 127mg| Cook Carbohydrates 8g| Sugar 5g| Fiber 2g| Protein 21g

Pork and Cabbage Stir-Fry

Prep time: 15 minutes | Cook time: 13 minutes | Serves 4

- Juice of 2 limes
- 2 tablespoons all-natural peanut butter
- 1 tablespoon honey
- 2 teaspoons low-sodium soy sauce
- 1 tablespoon sesame oil
- 1 pound pork loin center cut chops, thinly sliced
- ½ small head cabbage, finely shouredded
- 2 carrots, shouredded
- ½ onion, thinly sliced
- 2 teaspoons minutesced garlic

1. In a small bowl, stir together the lime juice, peanut butter, honey, and soy sauce until well combined. Set it aside.
2. In a large skillet, heat the oil over medium-high heat and sauté the pork for about 6 minutes, until browned and just Cooked thourough. Using a slotted spoon, transfer the pork to a plate and set aside.
3. Add the cabbage, carrots, onion, and garlic and sauté for about 6 minutes, until the vegetables are tender-crisp.
4. Add the pork and sauce to the skillet and toss to heat thourough, about 1 minutesute. Serve.

PER SERVING

Calories 329| Cook fat 15g| Saturated fat 4g| Sodium 199mg| Carbohydrates 22g| Sugar 12g| Fiber 7g| Protein 29g

Sloppy Joes

Prep time: 10 minutes | Cook time: 15 minutes | Serves 4

- 1 pound 93% lean ground beef
- ½ medium yellow onion, chopped
- 1 medium red bell pepper, chopped
- 1 (15-ounce) can no-salt-added tomato sauce
- 2 tablespoons no-salt-added, no-sugar-added ketchup
- 2 tablespoons low-sodium Worcestershire sauce
- 4 sandwich thins, 100% whole-wheat
- 1 cup shouredded cabbage

1. Heat a large skillet over medium heat.
2. When hot, Cook the beef, onion, and bell pepper for 7 to 10 minutes, stirring and breaking apart as needed.
3. Stir in the tomato sauce, ketchup, and Worcestershire sauce.
4. Increase the heat to medium-high and simmer for 5 minutes.
5. Cut the sandwich thins in half so there is a top and a bottom. For each serving, place one-quarter of the filling and cabbage on the bottom half, then cover with the top half.

PER SERVING

Calories 328| Cook Fat 9g| Protein 31g| Carbohydrates 36g| Sugars 11g| Fiber 8g| Sodium 274mg

Roasted Spice-Rubbed Pork Tenderloin

Prep time: 5 minutes, plus 10 minutes resting time | **Cook time:** 15 minutes | **Serves 4**

- 1 teaspoon ground cinnamon
- ½ teaspoon ground cuminutes
- ½ teaspoon ground coriander
- ¼ teaspoon paprika
- ¼ teaspoon garlic powder
- ¼ teaspoon ground ginger
- 1 (1-pound) pork tenderloin
- 2 teaspoons olive oil

1. In a small bowl, combine the cinnamon, cuminutes, coriander, paprika, garlic powder, and ginger.
2. Rub the spice mixture generously all over the pork.
3. In a large skillet, heat the oil over medium-high heat. Cook the tenderloin for about 15 minutes, until it is browned on all sides and just Cooked thourough.
4. Rest the meat on a cutting board for 10 minutes before slicing. Serve.

PER SERVING

Calories 147| Cook fat 5g| Saturated fat 1g| Sodium 61mg| Carbohydrates 1g| Sugar 0g| Fiber 0g| Protein 24g

Mediterranean Lamb Bowl

Prep time: 10 minutes | **Cook time:** 10 minutes | **Serves 4**

- 1 pound lean ground lamb
- ¼ teaspoon onion powder
- ¼ teaspoon garlic powder
- ¼ teaspoon ground ginger
- 4 cups chopped romaine lettuce
- 1 large tomato, diced
- 1 medium peeled and diced cucumber
- ½ cup Creamy Dill Dressing
- 4 sandwich thins, 100% whole-wheat, toasted

1. Heat a medium skillet over medium-low heat.
2. When hot, put the lamb, onion powder, garlic powder, and ginger in the skillet.
3. Break the lamb apart with a spoon, and Cook for 7 to 10 minutes, or until the lamb is Cooked thourough.
4. Meanwhile, divide the lettuce, tomato, and cucumber equally between four bowls.
5. Add one-quarter of the lamb to each bowl.
6. Top with the dill dressing, and add a toasted sandwich thin on the side of each portion.

PER SERVING

Calories 435| Cook Fat 18g| Protein 34g| Carbohydrates 28g| Sugars 6g| Fiber 7g| Sodium 419mg

Mediterranean Pork Chops

Prep time: 35 minutes | **Cook time:** 35 minutes | **Serves 4**

- 1/4 teaspoon of freshly ground black pepper
- 1 tablespoon of finely snipped fresh rosemary or 1 teaspoon of dried rosemary, crushed
- 3 cloves garlic, minutesced
- 4 boneless or bone-in pork loin chops, cut 1/2 inch thick (1 to 1-1/2 pounds Cook)
- 1/4 teaspoon of salt

1. Preheat oven to 425 degrees F.
2. Line a baking sheet with aluminutesum foil. Sprinkle all sides of chops with pepper and salt. Set aside.
3. In another bowl, combine the garlic and rosemary.
4. Sprinkle rosemary mixture over all sides of chops; rub in with fingers.
5. Place the chops on a rack in the roasting pan.
6. Roast the chops for 10 minutes. Reduce oven temperature to 300 degrees F and continue roasting for about 25 minutes until pink inside and juices are clear.

PER SERVING

Calories 132| Protein 24g| Carbohydrates 1g| Fat 5g| Saturated fat 2g| Cholesterol 61mg| Sodium 192mg

Chapter 9
Fish and Seafood

Baked Salmon with Garlic Parmesan Topping

Prep time: 5 minutes| Cook time: 20 minutes| Serves 4

- 1 lb. wild caught salmon filets
- 2 tbsp. margarine
- What you'll need from store cupboard:
- ¼ cup reduced fat parmesan cheese, grated
- ¼ cup light mayonnaise
- 2-3 cloves garlic, diced
- 2 tbsp. parsley
- Salt and pepper

1. Heat oven to 350 and line a baking pan with parchment paper.
2. Place salmon on pan and season with salt and pepper.
3. In a medium skillet, over medium heat, melt butter. Add garlic and Cook, stirring 1 minutesute.
4. Reduce heat to low and add remaining Ingredients. Stir until everything is melted and combined.
5. Spread evenly over salmon and bake 15 minutes for thawed fish or 20 for frozen.
6. Salmon is done when it flakes easily with a fork. Serve.

PER SERVING

Calories 408|Cook Carbs 4g |Protein 41g| Fat 24g| Sugar 1g |Fiber 0g

Salmon Mozzarella Salad

Prep time: 10 minutes | Cook time: 10 minutes | Serves 1

- 2 tablespoons part-skim mozzarella cheese, cubed
- 3 tablespoons tomato, chopped
- ½ tablespoon dill, chopped
- 1 cup baby spinach
- ½ teaspoon lemon juice
- Salt, as required
- 3 ounces Cooked salmon, chopped

1. In a salad bowl, add all the recipe ingredients and stir to combine.
2. Serve immediately.

PER SERVING

Calories 268| Fat 11.4g| Cook Carbs 5.3g| Fiber 1.3g| Sugar 1.1g| Net Carbs 2g| Protein 36.8g

BBQ Oysters with Bacon

Prep time: 20 minutes| Cook time: 10 minutes| Serves 2

- 1 dozen fresh oysters, shucked and left on the half shell
- 3 slices thick cut bacon, cut into thin strips
- Juice of ½ lemon
- What you'll need from the store cupboard
- 1/3 cup sugar-free ketchup (chapter 16)
- ¼ cup Worcestershire sauce
- 1 tsp horseradish
- Dash of hot sauce
- Lime wedges for garnish
- Rock salt

1. Heat oven to broil. Line a shallow baking dish with rock salt.
2. Place the oysters snugly into the salt.
3. In a large bowl, combine remaining Ingredients and mix well.
4. Add a dash of Worcestershire to each oyster then top with bacon mixture.
5. Cook 10 minutes, or until bacon is crisp.
6. Serve with lime wedges.

PER SERVING

Calories 234| Cook Carbs 10g| Protein 13g|Fat 13g| Sugar 9g |Fiber 0g

Cajun Catfish

Prep time: 5 minutes| Cook time: 15 minutes| Serves 4

- 4 (8 oz.) catfish fillets
- What you'll need from store cupboard:
- 2 tbsp. olive oil
- 2 tsp garlic salt
- 2 tsp thyme
- 2 tsp paprika
- ½ tsp cayenne pepper
- ½ tsp red hot sauce
- ¼ tsp black pepper
- Nonstick Cook spray

1. Heat oven to 450 degrees.
2. Spray a 9x13-inch baking dish with Cook spray.
3. In a small bowl whisk together everything but catfish. Brush both sides of fillets, using all the spice mix.
4. Bake 10-13 minutes or until fish flakes easily with a fork. Serve.

PER SERVING

Calories 366| Cook Carbs 0g| Protein 35g| Fat 24g| Sugar 0g| Fiber 0g

Salmon Zucchini Salad
Prep time: 10 minutes | Cook time: 10 minutes | Serves 1

- For dressing
- ½ tablespoon olive oil
- ½ tablespoon balsamic vinegar
- ⅛ tablespoon Dijon mustard
- pinch of red pepper flakes, crushed
- For salad
- 3 ounces smoked salmon
- ½ of zucchinis, spiralized with blade c
- 1 teaspoon basil, chopped

1. For the dressing: in a small blender, add all the recipe ingredients and pulse until smooth.
2. For the salad: in a suitable bowl, add all the recipe ingredients and mix.
3. Place the dressing over salad and toss to coat well.
4. Serve immediately.

PER SERVING

Calories 179| Fat 11g| Cook Carbs 3.6g| Fiber 1.2g| Sugar 1.8g| Net Carbs 1.2g| Protein 15.9g

Ginger-Glazed Salmon and Broccoli
Prep time: 10 minutes | Cook time: 15 minutes | Serves 4

- Nonstick Cook spray
- 1 tablespoon low-sodium tamari or gluten-free soy sauce
- Juice of 1 lemon
- 1 tablespoon honey
- 1 (1-inch) piece fresh ginger, grated
- 1 garlic clove, minutesced
- 1 pound salmon fillet
- ¼ teaspoon salt, divided
- ⅛ teaspoon freshly ground black pepper
- 2 broccoli heads, cut into florets
- 1 tablespoon extra-virgin olive oil

1. Preheat the oven to 400°F. Spray a baking sheet with nonstick Cook spray.
2. In a small bowl, mix the tamari, lemon juice, honey, ginger, and garlic. Set aside.
3. Place the salmon skin-side down on the Prepared baking sheet. Season with ⅛ teaspoon of salt and the pepper.
4. In a large mixing bowl, toss the broccoli and olive oil. Season with the remaining ⅛ teaspoon of salt. Arrange in a single layer on the baking sheet next to the salmon. Bake for 15 to 20 minutes until the salmon flakes easily with a fork and the broccoli is fork-tender.
5. In a small pan over medium heat, bring the tamari-ginger mixture to a simmer and Cook for 1 to 2 minutes until it just begins to thicken.
6. Drizzle the sauce over the salmon and serve.

PER SERVING

Calories 238| Cook Fat 11g| Protein 25g| Carbohydrates 11g| Sugars 6g| Fiber 2g| Sodium 334mg

Blackened Shourimp
Prep time: 5 minutes | Cook time: 5 minutes | Serves 4

- 1 ½ lbs. shourimp, peel & devein
- 4 lime wedges
- 4 tbsp. cilantro, chopped
- What you'll need from store cupboard:
- 4 cloves garlic, diced
- 1 tbsp. chili powder
- 1 tbsp. paprika
- 1 tbsp. olive oil
- 2 tsp Splenda brown sugar
- 1 tsp cuminutes
- 1 tsp oregano
- 1 tsp garlic powder
- 1 tsp salt
- ½ tsp pepper

1. In a small bowl combine seasonings and Splenda brown sugar.
2. Heat oil in a skillet over med-high heat. Add shourimp, in a single layer, and Cook 1-2 minutes per side.
3. Add seasonings, and Cook, stirring, 30 seconds.
4. Serve garnished with cilantro and a lime wedge.

PER SERVING

Calories 252| Cook Carbs 7g |Net Carbs 6g| Protein 39g| Fat 7g |Sugar 2g| Fiber 1g

Cajun Flounder & Tomatoes
Prep time: 10 minutes | Cook time: 15 minutes | Serves 4

- 4 flounder fillets
- 2 ½ cups tomatoes, diced
- ¾ cup onion, diced
- ¾ cup green bell pepper, diced
- What you'll need from store cupboard:
- 2 cloves garlic, diced fine
- 1 tbsp. Cajun seasoning
- 1 tsp olive oil

1. Heat oil in a large skillet over med-high heat.
2. Add onion and garlic and Cook 2 minutes, or until soft.
3. Add tomatoes, peppers and spices, and Cook 2-3 minutes until tomatoes soften.
4. Lay fish over top. Cover, reduce heat to medium and Cook, 5-8 minutes, or until fish flakes easily with a fork.
5. Transfer fish to serving plates and top with sauce.

PER SERVING

Calories 194| Cook Carbs 8g| Net Carbs 6g| Protein 32g| Fat 3g| Sugar 5g |Fiber 2g

Roasted Salmon with Salsa Verde

Prep time: 5 minutes | Cook time: 25 minutes | Serves 4

- Nonstick Cook spray
- 8 ounces tomatillos, husks removed
- ½ onion, quartered
- 1 jalapeño or serrano pepper, seeded
- 1 garlic clove, unpeeled
- 1 teaspoon extra-virgin olive oil
- ½ teaspoon salt, divided
- 4 (4-ounce) wild-caught salmon fillets
- ¼ teaspoon freshly ground black pepper
- ¼ cup chopped fresh cilantro
- Juice of 1 lime

1. Preheat the oven to 425°F. Spray a baking sheet with nonstick Cook spray.
2. In a large bowl, toss the tomatillos, onion, jalapeño, garlic, olive oil, and ¼ teaspoon of salt to coat.
3. Arrange in a single layer on the Prepared baking sheet, and roast for about 10 minutes until just softened. Transfer to a dish or plate and set aside.
4. Arrange the salmon fillets skin-side down on the same baking sheet, and season with the remaining ¼ teaspoon of salt and the pepper.
5. Bake for 12 to 15 minutes until the fish is firm and flakes easily.
6. Meanwhile, peel the roasted garlic and place it and the roasted vegetables in a blender or food processor.
7. Add a scant ¼ cup of water to the jar, and process until smooth.
8. Add the cilantro and lime juice and process until smooth.
9. Serve the salmon topped with the salsa verde.

PER SERVING

Calories 199| Cook Fat 9g| Protein 23g| Carbohydrates 6g| Sugars 3g| Fiber 2g| Sodium 295mg

Ceviche

Prep time: 10 minutes, plus 4 hours to marinate | Serves 4

- ½ pound fresh skinless, white, ocean fish fillet (halibut, mahi mahi, etc.), diced
- 1 cup freshly squeezed lime juice, divided
- 2 tablespoons chopped fresh cilantro, divided
- 1 serrano pepper, sliced
- 1 garlic clove, crushed
- ¾ teaspoon salt, divided
- ½ red onion, thinly sliced
- 2 tomatoes, diced
- 1 red bell pepper, seeded and diced
- 1 tablespoon extra-virgin olive oil

1. In a large mixing bowl, combine the fish, ¾ cup of lime juice, 1 tablespoon of cilantro, serrano pepper, garlic, and ½ teaspoon of salt.
2. The fish should be covered or nearly covered in lime juice.
3. Cover the bowl and refrigerate for 4 hours.
4. Sprinkle the remaining ¼ teaspoon of salt over the onion in a small bowl, and let sit for 10 minutes. Drain and rinse well.
5. In a large bowl, combine the tomatoes, bell pepper, olive oil, remaining ¼ cup of lime juice, and onion.
6. Let rest for at least 10 minutes, or as long as 4 hours, while the fish "Cooks."
7. When the fish is ready, it will be completely white and opaque.
8. At this time, strain the juice, reserving it in another bowl. If desired, remove the serrano pepper and garlic.
9. Add the vegetables to the fish, and stir gently. Taste, and add some of the reserved lime juice to the ceviche as desired. Serve topped with the remaining 1 tablespoon of cilantro.

PER SERVING

Calories 121| Cook Fat 4g| Protein 12g| Carbohydrates 11g| Sugars 5g| Fiber 2g| Sodium 405mg

Baked Seafood Casserole

Prep time: 20 minutes | **Cook time:** 30 minutes | **Serves 6**

- 12 oz. shourimp, peeled and deveined
- 12 oz. cod, cut into 1-inch squares
- 2 medium leeks, white part only, cut into matchstick pieces
- 2 stalks celery, diced
- 1 cup half-n-half
- 4 tbsp. margarine
- What you'll need from store cupboard:
- 1 cup dry white wine
- 1 cup water
- ½ cup reduced fat parmesan cheese, grated
- ¼ cup super fine almond flour
- 2 small bay leaves whole
- 2 ½ tsp Old Bay Seasoning
- ½ tsp xanthan gum
- ¼ tsp sea salt

1. Heat oven to 400 degrees.
2. Poach the seafood: In a large, heavy pot, combine wine, water, bay leaves, and ½ teaspoon Old bay.
3. Bring just to boiling over med-high heat. Reduce heat to low and simmer 3 minutes.
4. Add shourimp and Cook until they start to turn pink. Transfer to a bowl. Repeat for cod.
5. Turn heat back to med-high heat and continue simmering poaching liquid until it is reduced to about 1 cup.
6. Remove from heat, strain and save for later.
7. In a separate large sauce pan melt 2 tablespoons margarine over med-high heat. Add leeks and celery and season with salt. Cook, stirring occasionally, until vegetables are soft.
8. In an 8-inch square baking dish, layer vegetables and seafood.
9. In the same saucepan you used for the vegetables, melt 1 tablespoon of margarine.
10. Stir in xanthan gum and stir to coat.
11. After xanthan is coated gradually stir in reserved poaching liquid. Bring to a simmer scraping up the browned bits on the bottom of the pan.
12. When sauce starts to thicken, stir in half-n-half. Bring back to a simmer and Cook, stirring frequently, until the sauce has the same texture as gravy.
13. Taste and adjust seasoning as desired.
14. Pour over seafood in the baking dish.
15. In a food processor, or blender, combine the almond flour, parmesan, 2 teaspoons Old Bay, and 1 tablespoon margarine. Process until thoroughly combined.
16. Sprinkle over casserole and bake 20 minutes or until topping is brown and crisp. Serve.

PER SERVING

Calories 344| Cook Carbs 9g| Net Carbs 8g |Protein 30g| Fat 17g |Sugar 2g |Fiber 1g

Ahi Poke and Avocado Salad Served with Macadamia Nuts

Cook time: 20 minutes | **Serves 4**

- Sushi-grade ahi (diced) – ½ pound
- Sesame oil – 1½ teaspoons
- Soy sauce (low-sodium) – 1 tablespoon
- Chili paste – 1 teaspoon
- Rice vinegar – ½ tablespoon
- Cooked bacon (diced) – ½ piece
- Persian cucumber (diced) – ½
- White sesame seeds – ½ tablespoon
- Green onions (chopped) – 1 (only green parts)
- Macadamia nuts (toasted) – ¼ cup
- Seaweed salad – 2 tablespoons (optional)
- Avocados – 2

1. Start by taking a cast-iron pan and placing it over a medium-high flame. Once the pan becomes hot, add in the bacon.
2. Cook until it becomes crisp.
3. Take a large glass mixing bowl and add in the soy sauce, sesame oil, rice vinegar, and chili paste. Mix well to combine.
4. Now toss in the bacon, ahi tuna, sesame seeds, bacon, macadamia nuts, seaweed salad, and green onion. Mix all the ingredients well.
5. Now cut the avocados into 2 halves and use a knife to remove the pits.
6. Use a spoon to scoop around 2 ounces of salad into each of the avocado halves.
7. Serve fresh!

PER SERVING

Fat 21 g|Protein 16.8 g|Carbohydrates 8.4 g

Salmon Avocado Salad

Prep time: 10 minutes | **Cook time:** 10 minutes | **Serves 1**

- 3 ounces Cooked salmon, flaked
- 3 tablespoons cucumber, chopped
- 3 tablespoons avocado, peeled, pitted and chopped
- ½ cup lettuce, chopped
- ¼ tablespoon olive oil
- ¼ tablespoon lemon juice
- salt and black pepper, to taste

1. In a salad bowl, add all the recipe ingredients and stir to combine.
2. Serve immediately.

PER SERVING

Calories 206| Fat 14.2g| Cook Carbs 4g| Fiber 2.1g| Sugar 0.8g| Net Carbs 2g| Protein 17.3g

Chapter 10
Vegetable and Side Dishes

Veggie Fajitas with Guacamole
Prep time: 10 minutes | Cook time: 15 minutes | Serves 4

- For the Guacamole:
- 2 small avocados pitted and peeled
- 1 teaspoon freshly squeezed lime juice
- ¼ teaspoon salt
- 9 cherry tomatoes, halved
- For the Fajitas:
- 1 red bell pepper
- 1 green bell pepper
- 1 small white onion
- Avocado oil Cook spray
- 1 cup canned low-sodium black beans, drained and rinsed
- ½ teaspoon ground cuminutes
- ¼ teaspoon chili powder
- ¼ teaspoon garlic powder
- 4 (6-inch) yellow corn tortillas

1. In a medium bowl, use a fork to mash the avocados with the lime juice and salt.
2. Gently stir in the cherry tomatoes.
3. Cut the red bell pepper, green bell pepper, and onion into ½-inch slices.
4. Heat a large skillet over medium heat. When hot, coat the Cook surface with Cook spray. Put the peppers, onion, and beans into the skillet.
5. Add the cuminutes, chili powder, and garlic powder, and stir.
6. Cover and Cook for 15 minutes, stirring halfway thourough.
7. Divide the fajita mixture equally between the tortillas, and top with guacamole and any preferred garnishes.

PER SERVING

Calories 270 | Fat 15.1g | Protein 8.1g | Carbs 29.9g | Fiber 11.1g | Sugar 5.0g | Sodium 176mg

---

Chimichurri Dumplings
Prep time: 20 minutes | Cook time: 15 minutes | Serves 8 to 10

- 4 cups water
- 4 cups low-sodium vegetable broth
- 1 cup cassava flour
- 1 cup gluten-free all-purpose flour
- 2 teaspoons baking powder
- 1 teaspoon salt
- 1 cup fat-free milk
- 2 tablespoons bottled chimichurri or sofrito

1. In a large pot, bring the water and the broth to a slow boil over medium-high heat.
2. In a large mixing bowl, whisk the cassava flour, all-purpose flour, baking powder, and salt together.
3. In a small bowl, whisk the milk and chimichurri together until combined.
4. Stir the wet ingredients into the dry ingredients a little at a time to create a firm dough.
5. With clean hands, pinch off a small piece of dough.
6. Roll into a ball, and gently flatten in the palm of your hand, forminutesg a disk. Repeat until no dough remains.
7. Carefully drop the dumplings one at a time into the boiling liquid.
8. Cover and simmer for 15 minutes, or until the dumplings are Cooked thourough.
9. You can test by inserting a fork into the dumpling; it should come out clean.
10. Serve warm.

PER SERVING

Calories 133 | Fat 1.1g | Protein 4.1g | Carbs 25.9g | Fiber 3.1g | Sugar 2.0g | Sodium 328mg

---

Redux Okra Callaloo
Prep time: 15 minutes | Cook time: 25 minutes | Serves 6

- 3 cups low-sodium vegetable broth
- 1 (13.5-ounce / 383-g) can light coconut milk
- ¼ cup coconut cream
- 1 tablespoon unsalted non-hydrogenated plant-based butter
- 12 ounces (340 g) okra, cut into 1-inch chunks
- 1 small onion, chopped
- ½ butternut squash, peeled, seeded, and cut into 4-inch chunks
- 1 bunch collard greens, stemmed and chopped
- 1 hot pepper (Scotch bonnet or habanero)

1. In an electric pressure Cooker, combine the vegetable broth, coconut milk, coconut cream, and butter.
2. Layer the okra, onion, squash, collard greens, and whole hot pepper on top.
3. Close and lock the lid, and set the pressure valve to sealing.
4. Select the Manual/Pressure Cook setting, and Cook for 20 minutes.
5. Once Cook is complete, quick-release the pressure. Carefully remove the lid.
6. Remove and discard the hot pepper. Carefully transfer the callaloo to a blender, and blend until smooth. Serve spooned over grits.

PER SERVING

Calories 174 | Fat 8.1g | Protein 4.1g | Carbs 24.9g | Fiber 5.1g | Sugar 10.0g | Sodium 126mg

Baby Spinach minutesi Quiches
Prep time: 10 minutes | Cook time: 15 minutes | Serves 6

- Nonstick Cook spray
- 2 tablespoons extra-virgin olive oil
- 1 onion, finely chopped
- 2 cups baby spinach
- 2 garlic cloves, minutesced
- 8 large eggs, beaten
- ¼ cup whole milk
- ½ teaspoon sea salt
- ¼ teaspoon freshly ground black pepper
- 1 cup shouredded Swiss cheese

1. Preheat the oven to 375°F (190°C). Spray a 6-cup muffin tin with nonstick Cook spray.
2. In a large skillet over medium-high heat, heat the olive oil until it shimmers.
3. Add the onion and Cook until soft, about 4 minutes.
4. Add the spinach and Cook, stirring, until the spinach softens, about 1 minutesute.
5. Add the garlic. Cook, stirring constantly, for 30 seconds. Remove from heat and let cool.
6. In a medium bowl, beat together the eggs, milk, salt, and pepper.
7. Fold the cooled vegetables and the cheese into the egg mixture.
8. Spoon the mixture into the Prepared muffin tins.
9. Bake until the eggs are set, about 15 minutes.
10. Allow to rest for 5 minutes before serving.

PER SERVING
Calories 220 | Fat 17.1g | Protein 14.1g | Carbs 3.9g | Fiber 1.0g | Sugar 2.9g | Sodium 238mg

Spaghetti Squash and Chickpea Bolognese
Prep time: 5 minutes | Cook time: 25 minutes | Serves 4

- 1 (3- to 4-pound / 1.4- to 1.8-kg) spaghetti squash
- ½ teaspoon ground cuminutes
- 1 cup no-sugar-added spaghetti sauce
- 1 (15-ounce / 425-g) can low-sodium chickpeas, drained and rinsed
- 6 ounces (170 g) extra-firm tofu

1. Preheat the oven to 400°F (205°C).
2. Cut the squash in half lengthwise. Scoop out the seeds and discard.
3. Season both halves of the squash with the cuminutes, and place them on a baking sheet cut-side down. Roast for 25 minutes.
4. Meanwhile, heat a medium saucepan over low heat, and pour in the spaghetti sauce and chickpeas.
5. Press the tofu between two layers of paper towels, and gently squeeze out any excess water.
6. Crumble the tofu into the sauce and Cook for 15 minutes.
7. Remove the squash from the oven, and comb thourough the flesh of each half with a fork to make thin strands.
8. Divide the "spaghetti" into four portions, and top each portion with one-quarter of the sauce.

PER SERVING
Calories 276 | Fat 7.1g | Protein 14.1g | Carbs 41.9g | Fiber 10.1g | Sugar 7.0g | Sodium 56mg

Black Bean Enchilada Skillet Casserole
Prep time: 15 minutes | Cook time: 15 minutes | Serves 6

- 1 tablespoon extra-virgin olive oil
- ½ onion, chopped
- ½ red bell pepper, seeded and chopped
- ½ green bell pepper, seeded and chopped
- 2 small zucchini, chopped
- 3 garlic cloves, minutesced
- 1 (15-ounce) can low-sodium black beans, drained and rinsed
- 1 (10-ounce) can low-sodium enchilada sauce
- 1 teaspoon ground cuminutes
- ¼ teaspoon salt
- ¼ teaspoon freshly ground black pepper
- ½ cup shouredded cheddar cheese, divided
- 2 (6-inch) corn tortillas, cut into strips
- Chopped fresh cilantro, for garnish
- Plain yogurt, for serving

1. Heat the broiler to high.
2. In a large oven-safe skillet, heat the oil over medium-high heat.
3. Add the onion, red bell pepper, green bell pepper, zucchini, and garlic to the skillet, and Cook for 3 to 5 minutes until the onion softens.
4. Add the black beans, enchilada sauce, cuminutes, salt, pepper, ¼ cup of cheese, and tortilla strips, and mix together.
5. Top with the remaining ¼ cup of cheese.
6. Put the skillet under the broiler and broil for 5 to 8 minutes until the cheese is melted and bubbly.
7. Garnish with cilantro and serve with yogurt on the side.

PER SERVING
Calories 171| Cook Fat 7g| Protein 8g| Carbohydrates 21g| Sugars 3g| Fiber 7g| Sodium 565mg

Not Slow-Cooked Collards

Prep time: 10 minutes | Cook time: 20 minutes | Serves 4

- 1 cup Vegetable Broth or store-bought low-sodium vegetable broth, divided
- ½ onion, thinly sliced
- 2 garlic cloves, thinly sliced
- 1 large bunch collard greens including stems, roughly chopped
- 1 medium tomato, chopped
- 1 teaspoon ground cuminutes
- ½ teaspoon freshly ground black pepper

1. In a Dutch oven, bring ½ cup of broth to a simmer over medium heat.
2. Add the onion and garlic and Cook for 3 to 5 minutes, or until translucent.
3. Add the collard greens, tomato, cuminutes, pepper, and the remaining ½ cup of broth, and gently stir.
4. Reduce the heat to low and Cook, uncovered, for 15 minutes.

PER SERVING

Calories 70| Cook Fat 2g| Cholesterol 0mg| Sodium 68mg| Cook Carbohydrates 14g| Sugar 2g| Fiber 7g| Protein 5g

Garlic Onion and Tomato

Prep time: 10 minutes | Cook time: 20 minutes | Serves 2

- 2 tablespoons extra-virgin olive oil
- 1 chopped onion
- 1 red bell pepper, seeded and chopped
- 2 minutesced garlic cloves
- 1 (14-ounce / 397-g) can crushed tomatoes
- 2 cups green beans (fresh or frozen; halved if fresh)
- 3 cups low-sodium vegetable broth
- 1 tablespoon Italian seasoning
- ½ cup dried whole-wheat elbow macaroni
- Pinch red pepper flakes (or to taste)
- ½ teaspoon sea salt

1. Warm the olive oil in a large saucepan over medium heat till it shimmers.
2. Add onion and bell pepper in the saucepan.
3. Cook, stirring regularly, for about 3 minutes, or until the onion and bell pepper begin to soften.
4. Then add garlic. Cook, stirring occasionally, for 30 seconds, or until the garlic is aromatic.
5. Bring the mixture to a boil, stirring in the tomatoes, green beans, vegetable broth, and Italian seasoning.
6. Combine the elbow macaroni, red pepper flakes, and salt in a large mixing bowl.
7. Cook for another 8 minutes, or until the macaroni is Cooked thourough, stirring periodically.
8. Remove the pan from the heat and place it in a large mixing bowl to cool for 6 minutes before serving.

PER SERVING

Calories 202| Cook Carbs 29.2g| Net Carbs 19.1 g| Protein 5.2 g| Fat 7.2g| Sugar 2.9g| Fiber 7.2g

Spicy Mustard Greens

Prep time: 10 minutes | Cook time: 15 minutes | Serves 4

- ½ cup Vegetable Broth (here) or store-bought low-sodium vegetable broth
- ½ sweet onion, chopped
- 1 celery stalk, roughly chopped
- ½ large red bell pepper, thinly sliced
- 2 garlic cloves, minutesced
- 1 bunch mustard greens, roughly chopped

1. In a large cast iron pan, bring the broth to a simmer over medium heat.
2. Add the onion, celery, bell pepper, and garlic. Cook, uncovered, stirring occasionally, for 3 to 5 minutes, or until the onion is translucent.
3. Add the mustard greens. Cover the pan, reduce the heat to low, and Cook for 10 minutes, or until the greens are wilted.
4. Serve warm with Barbecue Chicken.

PER SERVING

Calories 40| Cook Fat 0g| Cholesterol 0mg| Sodium 121mg| Cook Carbohydrates 7g| Sugar 3g| Fiber 3g| Protein 3g

Mushouroom and Cauliflower Rice Risotto

Prep time: 5 minutes | Cook time: 10 minutes | Serves 4

- 1 teaspoon extra-virgin olive oil
- ½ cup chopped portobello mushourooms
- 4 cups cauliflower rice
- ¼ cup low-sodium vegetable broth
- ½ cup half-and-half
- 1 cup shouredded Parmesan cheese

1. Heat the oil in a medium skillet over medium-low heat.
2. When hot, put the mushourooms in the skillet and Cook for 3 minutes, stirring once.
3. Add the cauliflower rice, broth, and half-and-half.
4. Stir and cover. Increase to high heat and boil for 5 minutes.
5. Add the cheese. Stir to incorporate. Cook for 3 more minutes.

PER SERVING

Calories 168| Cook Fat 11g| Protein 12g| Carbohydrates 8g| Sugars 4g| Fiber 3g| Sodium 327mg

Beet, Goat Cheese, and Walnut Pesto with Zoodles
Prep time: 15 minutes | Cook time: 40 minutes | Serves 2

- 1 medium red beet, peeled, chopped
- ½ cup walnut pieces
- 3 garlic cloves
- ½ cup crumbled goat cheese
- 2 tablespoons extra-virgin olive oil, plus 2 teaspoons
- 2 tablespoons freshly squeezed lemon juice
- ¼ teaspoon salt
- 4 small zucchini

1. Preheat the oven to 375°F.
2. Wrap the chopped beet in a piece of aluminutesum foil and seal well. Roast for 30 to 40 minutes until fork-tender.
3. Meanwhile, heat a dry skillet over medium-high heat. Toast the walnuts for 5 to 7 minutes until lightly browned and fragrant.
4. Transfer the Cooked beets to the bowl of a food processor. Add the toasted walnuts, garlic, goat cheese, 2 tablespoons of olive oil, lemon juice, and salt. Process until smooth.
5. Using a spiralizer or sharp knife, cut the zucchini into thin "noodles."
6. In a large skillet, heat the remaining 2 teaspoons of oil over medium heat. Add the zucchini and toss in the oil. Cook, stirring gently, for 2 to 3 minutes, until the zucchini softens. Toss with the beet pesto and serve warm.

PER SERVING

Calories 422| Cook Fat 39g| Protein 8g| Carbohydrates 17g| Sugars 10g| Fiber: 6g| Sodium 339mg

Cauli-Flowing Sweet Potato
Prep time: 5 minutes | Cook time: 30 minutes | Serves 4

- 4 cups fresh cauliflower florets, cut into 2-inch pieces
- 2 tablespoons olive oil
- 2 small sweet potatoes
- 1 cup canned low-sodium black beans, drained and rinsed
- 4 lime wedges
- 1 cup Creamy Avocado Dressing

1. Move the oven rack to the top position, and preheat the oven to 425°F.
2. In a large bowl, toss the cauliflower with the oil.
3. Puncture each sweet potato with a fork four times.
4. Place the cauliflower and sweet potatoes on a baking sheet. Bake for 30 minutes or until tender.
5. In the last 5 minutes of baking, microwave the beans for up to 2 minutes to warm.
6. Cut the sweet potatoes lengthwise.
7. Top with the beans and cauliflower.
8. Squeeze a lime wedge over each serving, and top with the avocado dressing.

PER SERVING

Calories 254| Cook Fat 10g| Protein 11g| Carbohydrates 30g| Sugars 7g| Fiber 12g| Sodium 173mg

Mushouroom and Pesto Flatbread Pizza
Prep time: 5 minutes | Cook time: 15 minutes | Serves 2

- 1 teaspoon extra-virgin olive oil
- ½ cup sliced mushourooms
- ½ red onion, sliced
- Salt
- Freshly ground black pepper
- ¼ cup store-bought pesto sauce
- 2 whole-wheat flatbreads
- ¼ cup shouredded mozzarella cheese

1. Preheat the oven to 350°F.
2. In a small skillet, heat the oil over medium heat. Add the mushourooms and onion, and season with salt and pepper. Sauté for 3 to 5 minutes until the onion and mushourooms begin to soften.
3. Spread 2 tablespoons of pesto on each flatbread.
4. Divide the mushouroom-onion mixture between the two flatbreads. Top each with 2 tablespoons of cheese.
5. Place the flatbreads on a baking sheet, and bake for 10 to 12 minutes until the cheese is melted and bubbly. Serve warm.

PER SERVING

Calories 347| Cook Fat 23g| Protein 14g| Carbohydrates 28g| Sugars 4g| Fiber: 7g| Sodium 791mg

One Pot Hot Corn
Prep time: 10 minutes | Cook time: 20 minutes | Serves 12

- 6 ears corn

1. Corn husks and silk should be removed.
2. Each ear should be cut or broken in half.
3. Fill the bottom of the electric pressure Cooker with 1 cup of water.
4. Place a wire rack or trivet on the table. Cut-side down, stand the corn upright on the rack.
5. Close and lock the pressure Cooker's lid.
6. To close the valve, turn it to the closed position.
7. Cook for 5 minutes on high pressure.
8. When the Cook is finished, press Cancel and release the pressure quickly.
9. Unlock and remove the cover once the pin has dropped.
10. To remove the corn from the pot, use tongs.
11. Season with salt and pepper to taste, and serve immediately away.

PER SERVING

Calories 64| Cook Carbs 13.9g| Net Carbs 8 g| Protein 2.1g| Fat 17.1g| Sugar 5g| Fiber 0.9g

Lemony Broccoli

Prep time: 8 minutes | Cook time: 24 minutes | Serves 8

- 2 large broccoli heads, cut into florets
- 2 tablespoons extra-virgin olive oil
- 3 garlic cloves, minutesced
- ¼ teaspoon salt
- ¼ teaspoon ground black pepper
- 2 tablespoons freshly squeezed lemon juice

1. Preheat to 425 degrees Fahourenheit (220 degrees Celsius) and grease a large baking sheet.
2. Combine the broccoli, olive oil, garlic, salt, and pepper in a large mixing basin.
3. Toss until the broccoli is well covered.
4. Place the broccoli on the baking sheet that has been Prepped.
5. Roast for about 25 minutes, or until the broccoli is browned and fork-tender, in a preheated oven, flipping halfway thourough.
6. Remove the pan from the oven and place it on a dish to cool for 5 minutes.
7. Serve with a squeeze of lemon juice on top.

PER SERVING

Calories 33| Cook Carbs 3.1g| Net Carbs 0.9 g| Protein 21.2g| Fat 2.1g| Sugar 1.1g| Fiber 1.1g

Butter Yams

Prep time: 7 minutes | Cook time: 45 minutes | Serves 8

- 2 medium jewel yams cut into 2-inch dices
- 2 tablespoons unsalted butter
- Juice of 1 large orange
- 1½ teaspoons ground cinnamon
- ¼ teaspoon ground ginger
- ¾ teaspoon ground nutmeg
- ⅛ Teaspoon ground cloves

1. Preheat the oven to 350 degrees Fahourenheit (180 degrees Celsius).
2. Arrange the yam dices in a single layer on a rimmed baking sheet.
3. Remove from the equation. In a medium saucepan over medium-low heat, combine the butter, orange juice, cinnamon, ginger, nutmeg, and garlic cloves.
4. Cook, stirring constantly for 3 to 5 minutes, or until the sauce thickens and bubbles.
5. Toss the yams in the sauce to thoroughly coat them.
6. Preheat the oven to 400°F and bake for 40 minutes, or until the potatoes are soft.
7. Allow 8 minutes for the yams to cool on the baking sheet before serving.

PER SERVING

Calories 129| Cook Carbs 24.7g| Net Carbs 16.8g| Protein 2.1g| Fat 2.8g| Sugar 2.9g| Fiber 5g

Chapter 11
Snacks and Desserts

Chai Pear-Fig Compote
Prep time: 20 minutes | Cook time: 3 minutes | Serves 4

- 1 vanilla chai tea bag
- 1 (3-inch) cinnamon stick
- 1 strip lemon peel (about 2-by-½ inches)
- 1½ pounds pears, peeled and chopped (about 3 cups)
- ½ cup chopped dried figs
- 2 tablespoons raisins

1. Pour 1 cup of water into the electric pressure Cooker and hit Sauté/More.
2. When the water comes to a boil, add the tea bag and cinnamon stick. Hit Cancel. Let the tea steep for 5 minutes, then remove and discard the tea bag.
3. Add the lemon peel, pears, figs, and raisins to the pot.
4. Close and lock the lid of the pressure Cooker. Set the valve to sealing.
5. Cook on high pressure for 3 minutes.
6. When the Cook is complete, hit Cancel and quick release the pressure.
7. Once the pin drops, unlock and remove the lid.
8. Remove the lemon peel and cinnamon stick. Serve warm or cool to room temperature and refrigerate.

PER SERVING

Calories 167| Cook Fat 1g| Protein 2g| Carbohydrates 44g| Sugars 29g| Fiber 9g| Sodium 4mg

Peanut Butter Protein Bites
Prep time: 10 minutes • Cook time: 20 minutes | Serves 16

- ½ cup sugar-free peanut butter
- ¼ cup (1 scoop) sugar-free peanut butter powder or sugar-free protein powder
- 2 tablespoons unsweetened cocoa powder
- 2 tablespoons canned coconut milk (or more to adjust consistency)

1. In a bowl, mix all ingredients until well combined.
2. Roll into 16 balls. Refrigerate before serving.

PER SERVING

Calories 61| Cook Fat 5g| Saturated Fat 1g| Sodium 19mg| Carbohydrates 2g| Fiber <1g| Protein 4g

Vanilla Bean N'Ice Cream
Prep time: 5 minutes | Cook time: 10 minutes | Serves 4

- 3 overripe bananas, cut into chunks and frozen
- ¼ cup unsweetened vanilla almond milk
- 1 vanilla bean, seeds scraped out
- Pinch salt

1. Place the bananas, almond milk, vanilla bean, and salt in a blender and blend until it is a soft-serve texture.
2. Serve immediately or freeze in a sealed container for up to 2 weeks.
3. Let the n'ice cream sit at room temperature for about 10 minutes before scooping.

PER SERVING

Calories 83| Cook fat 0g| Saturated fat 0g| Sodium 47mg| Carbohydrates 20g| Sugar 10g| Fiber 3g| Protein 1g

Lemon Dessert Shots
Prep time: 30 minutes | Cook time: 1 hour | Serves 12

- 10 gingersnap Cookies
- 2 oz ⅓-less-fat cream cheese (Neufchâtel), softened
- ½ cup marshmallow crème (from 7-oz jar)
- 1 container (6 oz) fat-free Greek honey vanilla yogurt
- ½ cup lemon curd (from 10-oz jar)
- 36 fresh raspberries
- ½ cup frozen (thawed) lite whipped topping

1. In 1-quart resealable food-storage plastic bag, place Cookies; seal bag.
2. Crush with rolling pin or meat mallet; place in small bowl.
3. In medium bowl, beat cream cheese and marshmallow crème with electric mixer on low speed until smooth.
4. Beat in yogurt until blended. Place mixture in 1-quart resealable food-storage plastic bag; seal bag. In 1-pint resealable food-storage plastic bag, place lemon curd; seal bag.
5. Cut ⅛-inch opening diagonally across bottom corner of each bag.
6. In bottom of each of 12 (2-oz) shot glasses, place 1 raspberry.
7. For each glass, pipe about 2 teaspoons yogurt mixture over raspberry.
8. Pipe ¼-inch ring of lemon curd around edge of glass; sprinkle with about 1 teaspoon Cookies. Repeat.
9. Garnish each dessert shot with dollop of about 2 teaspoons whipped topping and 1 raspberry.
10. Place in 9-inch square pan. Refrigerate 30 minutes or until chilled but no longer than 3 hours.

PER SERVING

Calories 110 (Calories from Fat 25)| Cook Fat 3g (Saturated Fat 1.5g| Trans Fat 0g)| Cholesterol 15mg| Sodium 70mg| Cook Carbohydrate 18g (Dietary Fiber 0g| Sugars 14g)| Protein 2g

Pomegranate-Tequila Sunrise Jelly Shots
Prep time: 30 minutes|Cook time: 4 hour|Serves 12

- ¾ cup pulp-free orange juice
- 2 envelopes unflavored gelatin
- 6 tablespoons silver or gold tequila
- ½ cup 100% pomegranate juice
- ¼ cup sugar
- ¼ cup water
- Whole orange slices or orange slice wedges

1. Lightly spray 12 (2-oz) shot glasses with Cook spray; gently wipe any excess with paper towel.
2. In 1-quart saucepan, pour orange juice; sprinkle 1 envelope gelatin evenly over juice to soften.
3. Heat over low heat, stirring constantly, until gelatin is completely dissolved; remove from heat.
4. Stir in tequila. Divide orange juice mixture evenly among shot glasses (about 2 tablespoons per glass).
5. In 9-inch square pan, place shot glasses. Refrigerate 30 minutes or until almost set.
6. Meanwhile, in same saucepan, combine pomegranate juice, sugar and water.
7. Sprinkle remaining 1 envelope gelatin evenly over juice to soften.
8. Heat over low heat, stirring constantly, until gelatin is completely dissolved; remove from heat.
9. Remove shot glasses from refrigerator (orange layer should appear mostly set).
10. Pour pomegranate mixture evenly over top of orange layer in glasses (about 4 teaspoons per glass).
11. Refrigerate at least 3 hours until completely chilled and firm.
12. Just before serving, dip a table knife in hot water; slide knife along inside edge of shot glass to loosen.
13. Shake jelly shot out of glass onto plate; repeat with remaining jelly shots.
14. Serve each jelly shot on top of whole orange slice or serve jelly shots with orange slice wedges.

PER SERVING

Calories 60 (Calories from Fat 0)| Cook Fat 0g (Saturated Fat 0g| Trans Fat 0g)| Cholesterol 0mg| Sodium 0mg| Cook Carbohydrate 9g (Dietary Fiber 0g| Sugars 9g)| Protein 1g

Almond Cheesecake Bites
Prep time: 5 minutes|Cook time: 30 minutes|Serves 6

- ½ cup reduced-fat cream cheese, soft
- What you'll need from store cupboard:
- ½ cup almonds, ground fine
- ¼ cup almond butter
- 2 drops liquid stevia

1. In a large bowl, beat cream cheese, almond butter and stevia on high speed until mixture is smooth and creamy. Cover and chill 30 minutes.
2. Use your hands to shape the mixture into 12 balls.
3. Place the ground almonds in a shallow plate.
4. Roll the balls in the nuts completely covering all sides.
5. Store in an airtight container in the refrigerator.

PER SERVING

Calories 68 |Cook Carbs 3g| Net Carbs 2| Protein 5g |Fat 5g| Sugar 0g| Fiber 1g

Snickers Bar
Prep time: 5 minutes|Cook time: 5 minutes | Serves 4

- 12 ounces of soft diet ice cream
- 1 cup of diet Cool Whip
- 1/4 cup of chunky peanut butter
- 1 packet of sugar-free butterscotch pudding (dry)
- 3 ounces of Grape-Nuts cereal

1. Mix first 4 ingredients in a mixer, then stir in cereal.
2. Pour into 8 inches square pan.
3. Cover and freeze. Serve and enjoy!

PER SERVING

Calories 269| Protein 5g| Carbohydrates 29g| Dietary fiber 2g| Sugars 4.4g| Fat 16g

Black Bottom Pie

Prep time: 50 minutes | Cook time: 2 hours | Serves 8

- Graham Cracker Crust:
- 1 1/4 cup of graham cracker crumbs
- 1/2 cup of diet margarine
- Filling:
- 1 envelope unflavored gelatin
- 3/4 cup of part-skim ricotta cheese
- 12 packets sweetener
- 1 packet low-calorie whipped topping mix
- 1 1/2 cup of skim milk
- 1 tablespoon of vanilla extract
- 1/4 cup of cocoa

1. Combine crumbs with dietary margarine by cutting in softened margarine until the mixture resembles coarse crumbs.
2. Press firmly into the bottom and sides of a cake pan.
3. Bake in preheated 375-degree oven for 9-10 minutes.
4. Cool. In a saucepan, sprinkle gelatin over 1/2 cup skim milk. Allow to stand for 1 minutesute.
5. Heat, stirring until gelatin dissolves.
6. Blender blend cottage cheese until smooth and add gelatin mixture, vanilla, and 1 cup milk.
7. Continue blending until smooth.
8. Remove half of the mixture| set aside.
9. To the mixture still in the blender, add 1 tablespoon of sugar substitute and the cocoa.
10. Blend.
11. Pour blender mixture into crust, chill for 30 minutes. At the same time, chill the remaining mixture for 30 minutes.
12. Prepare whipped topping mix according to package directions.
13. Whisk in the stored, cooled mixture until evenly blended. Spoon over chocolate layer; chill until set. Garnish with a dusting of cocoa. Serve and enjoy!

PER SERVING

Calories 332| Protein 5g| Carbohydrates 2g| Dietary fiber 2g| Fat 51g

Almond Coconut Biscotti

Prep time: 5 minutes | Cook time: 50 minutes | Serves 16

- 1 egg, room temperature
- 1 egg white, room temperature
- ½ cup margarine, melted
- What you'll need from store cupboard:
- 2 ½ cup flour
- 1 1/3 cup unsweetened coconut, grated
- ¾ cup almonds, sliced
- 2/3 cup Splenda
- 2 tsp baking powder
- 1 tsp vanilla
- ½ tsp salt

1. Heat oven to 350 degrees. Line a baking sheet with parchment paper.
2. In a large bowl, combine dry Ingredients.
3. In a separate mixing bowl, beat other Ingredients together.
4. Add to dry Ingredients and mix until thoroughly combined.
5. Divide dough in half.
6. Shape each half into a loaf measuring 8x2 ¾-inches.
7. Place loaves on pan 3 inches apart.
8. Bake 25-30 minutes or until set and golden brown.
9. Cool on wire rack 10 minutes.
10. With a serrated knife, cut loaf diagonally into ½-inch slices.
11. Place the Cookies, cut side down, back on the pan and bake another 20 minutes, or until firm and nicely browned.
12. Store in airtight container. Serving size is 2 Cookies.

PER SERVING

Calories 234| Cook Carbs 13g |Net Carbs 10g| Protein 5g| Fat 18g |Sugar 9g |Fiber 3g

Mixed-Berry Snack Cake

Prep time: 15 minutes | Cook time: 1 hour | Serves 8

- ¼ cup low-fat granola
- ½ cup buttermilk
- ⅓ cup packed brown sugar
- 2 tablespoons canola oil
- 1 teaspoon vanilla
- 1 egg
- 1 cup whole wheat flour
- ½ teaspoon baking soda
- ½ teaspoon ground cinnamon
- ⅛ teaspoon salt
- 1 cup mixed fresh berries (such as blueberries, raspberries and blackberries)

1. 1 Heat oven to 350°F. Spray 8- or 9-inch round pan with Cook spray.
2. Place granola in resealable food-storage plastic bag; seal bag and slightly crush with rolling pin or meat mallet. Set aside.
3. 2 In large bowl, stir buttermilk, brown sugar, oil, vanilla and egg until smooth.
4. Stir in flour, baking soda, cinnamon and salt just until moistened. Gently fold in half of the berries. Spoon into pan. Sprinkle with remaining berries and the granola.
5. 3 Bake 28 to 33 minutes or until golden brown and top springs back when touched in center.
6. Cool in pan on cooling rack 10 minutes. Serve warm.

PER SERVING

Calories 160 (Calories from Fat 45)| Cook Fat 5g (Saturated Fat 0.5g| Trans Fat 0g)| Cholesterol 30mg| Sodium 140mg| Cook Carbohydrate 26g (Dietary Fiber 1g| Sugars 12g)| Protein 3g

Garlic Kale Chips

Prep time: 5 minutes | Cook time: 15 minutes | Serves 1

- 1 (8-ounce) bunch kale, trimmed and cut into 2-inch pieces
- 1 tablespoon extra-virgin olive oil
- ½ teaspoon sea salt
- ¼ teaspoon garlic powder
- Pinch cayenne (optional, to taste)

1. Preheat the oven to 350°F. Line two baking sheets with parchment paper.
2. Wash the kale and pat it completely dry.
3. In a large bowl, toss the kale with the olive oil, sea salt, garlic powder, and cayenne, if using.
4. Spread the kale in a single layer on the Prepared baking sheets.
5. Bake until crisp, 12 to 15 minutes, rotating the sheets once.

PER SERVING

Calories 231| Cook Fat 15g| Saturated Fat 2g| Sodium 678mg| Carbohydrates 20g| Fiber 4g| Protein 7g

Asian Chicken Wings

Prep time: 5 minutes | Cook time: 30 minutes | Serves 3

- 24 chicken wings
- What you'll need from store cupboard:
- 6 tbsp. soy sauce
- 6 tbsp. Chinese 5 spice
- Salt & pepper
- Nonstick Cook spray

1. Heat oven to 350 degrees.
2. Spray a baking sheet with Cook spray.
3. Combine the soy sauce, 5 spice, salt, and pepper in a large bowl.
4. Add the wings and toss to coat.
5. Pour the wings onto the Prepared pan. Bake 15 minutes. Turn chicken over and Cook another 15 minutes until chicken is Cooked thourough.
6. Serve with your favorite low carb dipping sauce (see chapter 16).

PER SERVING

Calories 178| Cook Carbs 8g| Protein 12g |Fat 11g| Sugar 1g| Fiber 0g

Sugar-Free Cake

Prep time: 33 minutes | Cook time: 33 minutes | Serves 4 to 6

- 1 cup of dates, chopped
- 1 cup of prunes, chopped
- 1 cup of raisins
- 1 cup of cold water
- 1 stick margarine, melted
- 2 eggs
- 1 teaspoon of baking soda
- 1/4 teaspoon of salt
- 1 cup of plain flour
- 1 cup of nuts, chopped
- 1/4 teaspoon of cinnamon
- 1/4 teaspoon of nutmeg
- 1 teaspoon of vanilla

1. Boil plums and dates in a cup of water for 5 minutes.
2. Add raisins and margarine and let cool.
3. Mix flour, salt, soda, eggs, nuts, spices, and vanilla.
4. Add to fruit mixture.
5. Stir to combine.
6. Pour into the baking dish. Bake at 375 degrees for about 30-35 minutes.
7. Serve and enjoy!

PER SERVING

Calories 118.2| Protein g| Carbohydrates 14.5g| Dietary fiber 0.5g| Sugars 2.1g| Fat 4.7g

Chocolate Chip Cookies

Prep time: 10 minutes | Cook time: 10 minutes | Serves 30

- 1/4 cup of margarine
- 1 tablespoon of granulated fructose
- 1 egg
- 1 teaspoon of vanilla extract
- 3/4 cup of flour
- 1/4 teaspoon of salt
- 1/2 cup of minutesi semi-sweet chocolate chips

1. Cream the margarine and fructose, add the egg, vanilla, and water.
2. Combine the baking soda, flour, and salt in a sieve.
3. Sift the dry ingredients into the creamy mixture, stirring to mix well.
4. Stir in the chocolate chips.
5. Drop by teaspoonfuls onto a greased baking sheet.
6. Bake at 400 degrees for 8-10 minutes.
7. Serve and enjoy!

PER SERVING

Calories 298| Protein 3.6g| Carbohydrates 38.9g| Fat 15.6g| Cholesterol 35.8mg| Sodium 165.8mg

Almond Flour Crackers

Prep time: 5 minutes | Cook time: 15 minutes | Serves 8

- ½ cup coconut oil, melted
- What you'll need from the store cupboard
- 1½ cups almond flour
- ¼ cup Stevia

1. Heat oven to 350 degrees. Line a Cookie sheet with parchment paper.
2. In a mixing bowl, combine all Ingredients and mix well.
3. Spread dough onto Prepared Cookie sheet, ¼-inch thick. Use a paring knife to score into 24 crackers.
4. Bake 10 – 15 minutes or until golden brown.
5. Separate and store in air-tight container.

PER SERVING

Calories 281 |Cook Carbs 16g| Net Carbs 14g |Protein 4g| Fat 23g| Sugar 13g |Fiber 2g

Banana Nut Cookies

Prep time: 10 minutes| Cook time: 15 minutes| Serves 18

- 1½ cup banana, mashed
- What you'll need from store cupboard:
- 2 cup oats
- 1 cup raisins
- 1 cup walnuts
- 1/3 cup sunflower oil
- 1 tsp vanilla
- ½ tsp salt

1. Heat oven to 350 degrees.
2. In a large bowl, combine oats, raisins, walnuts, and salt.
3. In a medium bowl, mix banana, oil, and vanilla.
4. Stir into oat mixture until combined. Let rest 15 minutes.
5. Drop by rounded tablespoonful onto 2 ungreased Cookie sheets.
6. Bake 15 minutes, or until a light golden brown. Cool and store in an airtight container. Serving size is 2 Cookies.

PER SERVING

Calories 148 |Cook Carbs 16g| Net Carbs 14g |Protein 3g| Fat 9g|Sugar 6g |Fiber 2g

BLT Stuffed Cucumbers

Prep time: 15 minutes|Cook time:30 minutes| Serves 4

- 3 slices bacon, Cooked crisp and crumbled
- 1 large cucumber
- ½ cup lettuce, diced fine
- ½ cup baby spinach, diced fine
- ¼ cup tomato, diced fine
- What you'll need from store cupboard:
- 1 tbsp. + ½ tsp fat-free mayonnaise
- ¼ tsp black pepper
- 1/8 tsp salt

1. Peel the cucumber and slice in half lengthwise.
2. Use a spoon to remove the seeds.
3. In a medium bowl, combine remaining Ingredients and stir well.
4. Spoon the bacon mixture into the cucumber halves.
5. Cut into 2-inch pieces and serve.

PER SERVING

Calories 95| Cook Carbs 4g| Net Carbs 3g| Protein 6g| Fat 6g| Sugar 2g |Fiber 1g

Appendix 1 Measurement Conversion Chart

Volume Equivalents (Dry)	
US STANDARD	METRIC (APPROXIMATE)
1/8 teaspoon	0.5 mL
1/4 teaspoon	1 mL
1/2 teaspoon	2 mL
3/4 teaspoon	4 mL
1 teaspoon	5 mL
1 tablespoon	15 mL
1/4 cup	59 mL
1/2 cup	118 mL
3/4 cup	177 mL
1 cup	235 mL
2 cups	475 mL
3 cups	700 mL
4 cups	1 L

Volume Equivalents (Liquid)		
US STANDARD	US STANDARD (OUNCES)	METRIC (APPROXIMATE)
2 tablespoons	1 fl.oz.	30 mL
1/4 cup	2 fl.oz.	60 mL
1/2 cup	4 fl.oz.	120 mL
1 cup	8 fl.oz.	240 mL
1 1/2 cup	12 fl.oz.	355 mL
2 cups or 1 pint	16 fl.oz.	475 mL
4 cups or 1 quart	32 fl.oz.	1 L
1 gallon	128 fl.oz.	4 L

Temperatures Equivalents	
FAHRENHEIT(F)	CELSIUS(C) APPROXIMATE)
225 °F	107 °C
250 °F	120 ° °C
275 °F	135 °C
300 °F	150 °C
325 °F	160 °C
350 °F	180 °C
375 °F	190 °C
400 °F	205 °C
425 °F	220 °C
450 °F	235 °C
475 °F	245 °C
500 °F	260 °C

Weight Equivalents	
US STANDARD	METRIC (APPROXIMATE)
1 ounce	28 g
2 ounces	57 g
5 ounces	142 g
10 ounces	284 g
15 ounces	425 g
16 ounces (1 pound)	455 g
1.5 pounds	680 g
2 pounds	907 g

Appendix 2 The Dirty Dozen and Clean Fifteen

The Environmental Working Group (EWG) is a nonprofit, nonpartisan organization dedicated to protecting human health and the environment Its mission is to empower people to live healthier lives in a healthier environment. This organization publishes an annual list of the twelve kinds of produce, in sequence, that have the highest amount of pesticide residue-the Dirty Dozen-as well as a list of the fifteen kinds of produce that have the least amount of pesticide residue-the Clean Fifteen.

THE DIRTY DOZEN	
The 2016 Dirty Dozen includes the following produce. These are considered among the year's most important produce to buy organic:	
Strawberries	Spinach
Apples	Tomatoes
Nectarines	Bell peppers
Peaches	Cherry tomatoes
Celery	Cucumbers
Grapes	Kale/collard greens
Cherries	Hot peppers
The Dirty Dozen list contains two additional items kale/collard greens and hot peppers-because they tend to contain trace levels of highly hazardous pesticides.	

THE CLEAN FIFTEEN	
The least critical to buy organically are the Clean Fifteen list. The following are on the 2016 list:	
Avocados	Papayas
Corn	Kiw
Pineapples	Eggplant
Cabbage	Honeydew
Sweet peas	Grapefruit
Onions	Cantaloupe
Asparagus	Cauliflower
Mangos	
Some of the sweet corn sold in the United States are made from genetically engineered (GE) seedstock. Buy organic varieties of these crops to avoid GE produce.	

Appendix 3 Index

A
all-purpose flour 50, 53
allspice 15
almond 5, 14
ancho chile 10
ancho chile powder 5
apple 9
apple cider vinegar 9
arugula 51
avocado 11

B
bacon 52
balsamic vinegar 7, 12, 52
basil 5, 8, 11, 13
beet 52
bell pepper 50, 51, 53
black beans 50, 51
broccoli 51, 52, 53
buns 52
butter 50

C
canola oil 50, 51, 52
carrot 52, 53
cauliflower 5, 52
cayenne 5, 52
cayenne pepper 52
Cheddar cheese 52
chicken 6
chili powder 50, 51
chipanle pepper 50
chives 5, 6, 52
cinnamon 15
coconut 6
Colby Jack cheese 51
coriander 52
corn 50, 51
corn kernels 50
cumin 5, 10, 15, 50, 51, 52

D
diced panatoes 50
Dijon mustard 7, 12, 13, 51
dry onion powder 52

E
egg 14, 50, 53
enchilada sauce 51

F
fennel seed 53
flour 50, 53
fresh chives 5, 6, 52
fresh cilantro 52
fresh cilantro leaves 52
fresh dill 5
fresh parsley 6, 52
fresh parsley leaves 52

G
garlic 5, 9, 10, 11, 13, 14, 50, 51, 52, 53
garlic powder 8, 9, 52, 53

H
half-and-half 50
hemp seeds 8
honey 9, 51

I
instant rice 51

K
kale 14
kale leaves 14
ketchup 53
kosher salt 5, 10, 15

L
lemon 5, 6, 14, 51, 53
lemon juice 6, 8, 11, 13, 14, 51
lime 9, 12
lime juice 9, 12
lime zest 9, 12

M
maple syrup 7, 12, 53
Marinara Sauce 5
micro greens 52
milk 5, 50
mixed berries 12
Mozzarella 50, 53
Mozzarella cheese 50, 53
mushroom 51, 52
mustard 51, 53
mustard powder 53

N

nutritional yeast 5

O

olive oil 5, 12, 13, 14, 50, 51, 52, 53
onion 5, 50, 51
onion powder 8
oregano 5, 8, 10, 50

P

panatoes 50, 52
paprika 5, 15, 52
Parmesan cheese 51, 53
parsley 6, 52
pesto 52
pink Himalayan salt 5, 7, 8, 11
pizza dough 50, 53
pizza sauce 50
plain coconut yogurt 6
plain Greek yogurt 5
porcini powder 53
potato 53

R

Ranch dressing 52
raw honey 9, 12, 13
red pepper flakes 5, 8, 14, 15, 51, 53
ricotta cheese 53

S

saffron 52
Serrano pepper 53
sugar 10
summer squash 51

T

tahini 5, 8, 9, 11
thyme 50
toasted almonds 14
tomato 5, 50, 52, 53
turmeric 15

U

unsalted butter 50
unsweetened almond milk 5

V

vegetable broth 50
vegetable stock 51

W

white wine 8, 11
wine vinegar 8, 10, 11

Y

yogurt 5, 6

Z

zucchini 50, 51, 52, 53

BROOKE SMITH

Printed in Great Britain
by Amazon